VIDEO
GAMES

VIDEO GAMES

FROM PONG
TO THE PS5

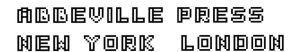

ABBEVILLE PRESS
NEW YORK LONDON

NICOLÒ MULAS MARCELLO
ALBERTO BERTOLAZZI

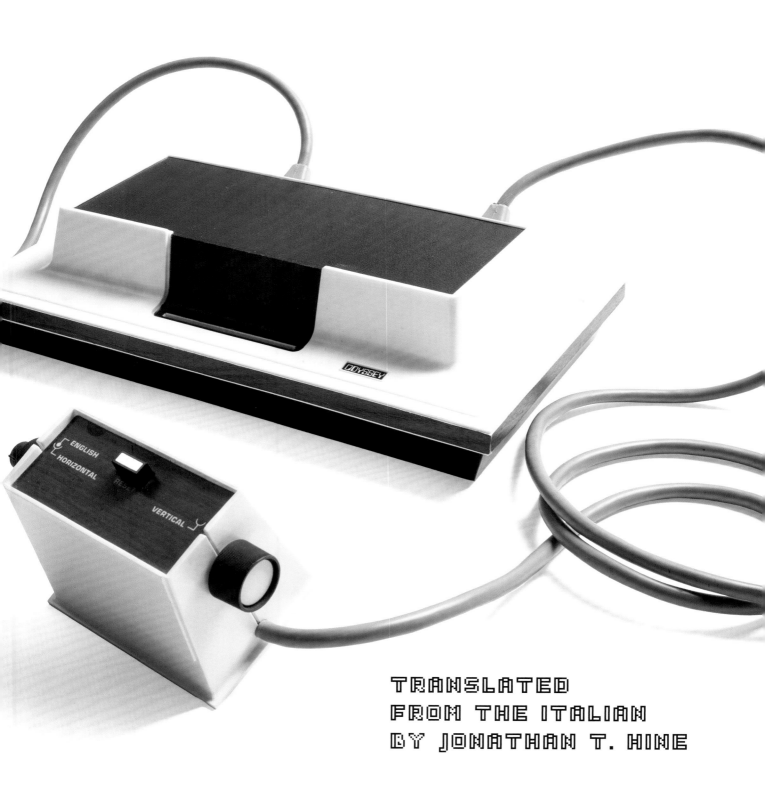

TRANSLATED
FROM THE ITALIAN
BY JONATHAN T. HINE

VIDEOGAME ART MUSEUM

Published in collaboration with the **Videogame Art Museum**, Bologna

PAGES 2–3: The Magnavox Odyssey console (1972).

ABOVE: The Valve Steam Controller (2015).

OPPOSITE: The QuickShot II joystick (1983).

PAGES 6–7: The Video Battle Centre, one of London's most famous gaming arcades, in the heart of Soho in 1979.

ABOUT THE AUTHORS

Nicolò Mulas Marcello is an independent journalist who has written for various local and national publications in Italy. A fan of video games since childhood, he owns a two-thousand-piece collection that includes consoles, computers, games, and memorabilia. Since 2018, he has been president of the Associazione Insert Coin, which operated the Videogame Art Museum in Bologna.

Alberto Bertolazzi has written for numerous publications in Italy and has authored many books on sports and technology, including a biography of Steve Jobs. He made his fiction debut in 2011 with *Il rugby salverà il mondo* (Rugby Will Save the World).

For the original edition
Editor: Federica Romagnoli
Designer: Elena Tomasino
Copy editor: Paolo Biano
Proofreader: Marilde Quaranta
Web support: Paolo Biano
Special thanks: Fabrizio Danieli

This book was first published in the English language in 2024 by Abbeville Press, 655 Third Avenue, Suite 2520, New York, NY 10017. It was translated from the Italian edition published in 2022 by Nuinui SA, Chemin du Tsan du Pèri 10, 3971 Chermignon, Switzerland.

First edition • 10 9 8 7 6 5 4 3 2 1

ISBN 978-0-7892-1485-0

Library of Congress Cataloging-in-Publication Data available upon request

For bulk and premium sales and for text adoption procedures, write to Customer Service Manager, Abbeville Press, 655 Third Avenue, New York, NY 10017, or call 1-800-Artbook.

Visit Abbeville Press online at www.abbeville.com.

CONTENTS

The history of video games is customarily divided into successive generations of consoles. Each chapter of this book covers one such generation.

INTRODUCTION
FROM THE OSCILLOSCOPE TO VIRTUAL REALITY

From *OXO* in 1952 to *Plague Inc.*, the prophetic pre-COVID title, the history of video games has revolved around the gaming experience. The improvement in immersiveness (from arcade cabinets to the total engagement of VR headsets) has gone hand in hand with the increase in computing power needed for fluid movement and scenery, with the portability (and thus miniaturization) of the consoles, with the tactile performance of the controllers, with better storytelling and the spread of online multiplayer games. Each step, each success— but also each failure—has brought gaming into the lives of millions of people, building an industry worth billions of dollars but, more importantly, a cultural, social, and educational phenomenon, which in its best expression may be considered the Eighth Art.

THE 1950S + 1960S
THE FIRST EXPERIMENTS

The Big Bang of video gaming began with the advent of the first electronic computers. Enormous boxes full of flashing lights and buttons, filling entire rooms, stimulated the genius of the habitués of universities and research centers. Cambridge, 1952: for his PhD dissertation on the interaction between human and machine, Alexander Douglas programs *OXO*—and the first electronic game on a phosphorescent screen enters history. In an experiment far ahead of its time, Douglas challenged the mammoth EDSAC computer to a game of tic-tac-toe using a rotary telephone dial to send commands.

A few years later, in 1958, the American physicist William Higinbotham invented *Tennis for Two*—recognized as the first video game created purely for entertainment. Using an oscilloscope and two rudimentary joysticks, it was possible to simulate the bounce of a ball on a tennis court with a luminous dot.

The height of the Cold War also affected the world of video gaming. The space race was a popular obsession. Thus, while Yuri Gagarin was completing the first orbit of Earth in 1961, MIT student Steve Russell and some classmates used the powerful PDP-1 computer at their university to program a video game that simulated a duel between two spaceships: *Spacewar!*

THE 1970S
ADVENT OF THE ARCADES

In 1971, inspired by the potential of *Spacewar!*, the engineer Nolan Bushnell brought out *Computer Space*, the first coin-operated video game in history. In 1969, Neil Armstrong had stepped onto the moon, and young people had become even more fascinated with distant worlds. The little spaceship in the arcade cabinet could move freely in the immensity of outer space, following the laws of physics and shooting at enemy ships. The following year, Bushnell and his partner Ted Dabney launched the video game industry by founding the historic company Atari. In 1972, the firm released *Pong*, the first real arcade hit. As in ping-pong, two players could launch the ball into each other's court, trying to rack up points.

That same year, 1972, also saw the release of the first home console: the Magnavox Odyssey, created by the engineer Ralph Baer, which offered table tennis and some variants. In 1977, Apple began the era of the home computer, while Atari became the leader of the home console market with the Atari 2600. The games were very simple, both in graphics and narrative structure, but thanks to the interchangeable cartridge, Atari sold 30 million consoles worldwide.

Following Atari, other companies developed video games for the arcades. For example, *Space Invaders* (1978), by the Japanese firm Taito, signaled the beginning of the golden age of arcades. These venues played a fundamental role in supporting the video gaming industry and became a refuge for millions of kids around the world. The quality of console games still had a long way to go to match the arcade versions of the same titles. It was not a matter of computing power per se, but of storage: an arcade game could be hardwired into numerous chips on a motherboard as big as a tabloid sheet of paper, while a home console game needed to fit into a small cartridge. This placed real limits on graphics quality, and only in later years would miniaturization bear its fruit.

THE 1980S
CRISIS + RENAISSANCE

Unconventional, colorful, and reckless, the eighties produced some of the most iconic titles in video gaming history. *Pac-Man* (1980), *Donkey Kong* (1981), and *Tetris* (1984) were among the releases that contributed to the spread of video games around the world. However, 1983 will be remembered as a year of crisis for the American video game market. Bankruptcy threatened many companies, including Atari. Too many low-quality games were flooding the market, falling short of the expectations of the ever more discerning video gamers. Many video games were inspired by blockbuster movies, like the *Star Wars* saga, but that was no guarantee of quality. *E.T. The Extra-Terrestrial* (1982) was a historic flop, considered the worst video game of all time. Unsatisfactory graphics and confusing gameplay annoyed many users, who demanded refunds. The development of video game cartridges and the adaptation of arcade games for consoles became ever more rushed and of ever lower quality, inexorably driving down the fortunes of the video gaming world. In that same year, 1982, the Commodore 64 was released, and became the best-selling computer in the world.

The collapse of the American video game industry made room for the Japanese and the era of the 8-bit machines. The Nintendo Entertainment System (NES) conquered the market with *Super Mario Bros.* (1985). The mustachioed Italian-American plumber radically changed the concept of the video game with its extraordinary innovations: for example, the side-scrolling platform, the ability to transform and power up, and the discovery of secret levels. The animated sprites—that is, the two-dimensional objects moving across the video game background—were better defined, and rekindled kids' enthusiasm for video gaming. But another innovation in gameplay was also key in getting millions of young people to challenge each other in front of the TV set: the joypad. The NES joypad was especially well designed. Its very simplicity—a directional cross and two buttons—made movement more precise, improved handling, and allowed combinations of keystrokes. To better understand the sales figures for *Super Mario Bros*, simply compare them with those of the hit single "We Are The World," by the group USA for Africa (Michael Jackson, Lionel Ritchie, Stevie Wonder, Bob Dylan, Bruce Springsteen and others), which sold 20 million copies worldwide in 1985. The *Super Mario* cartridge, released in the same year, sold 40 million copies.

The end of the decade was marked by the portable revolution driven by the Game Boy (1989), with which Nintendo dominated the market for years. SEGA also decided to offer the world its own consoles—first the Master System (1986) and then the Mega Drive (1988)—starting a historic commercial war with its rival, Nintendo.

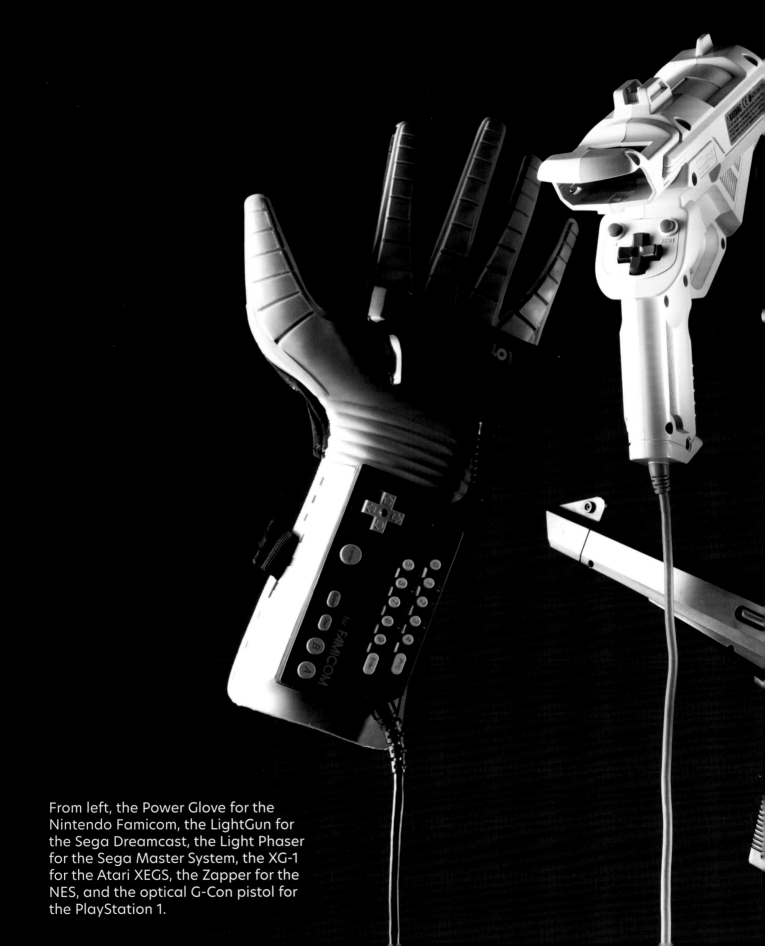

From left, the Power Glove for the Nintendo Famicom, the LightGun for the Sega Dreamcast, the Light Phaser for the Sega Master System, the XG-1 for the Atari XEGS, the Zapper for the NES, and the optical G-Con pistol for the PlayStation 1.

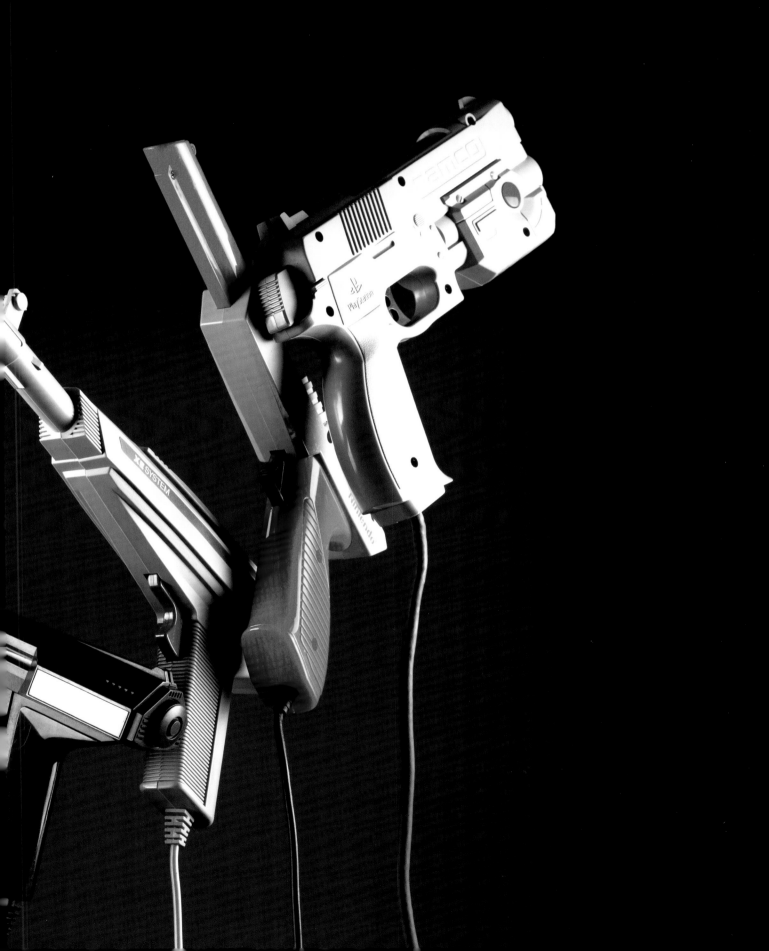

THE 1990S
THE THIRD DIMENSION

The fall of the Berlin Wall opened a decade whose events have reverberated down to the present: the wars in the Persian Gulf and the Balkans; the Treaty of Maastricht, which made the European Union a reality; the liberation of Nelson Mandela and the end of South African apartheid; but also cultural phenomena like the Spice Girls, boy bands, grunge, and the spread of Tamagotchi and karaoke.

Much also changed in video gaming. Hardware innovations in consoles followed in rapid succession, beginning with the 16-bit Super Nintendo (1990) and Sega Mega Drive (1988), continuing with the 32-bit 3DO (1993), and arriving finally at the extraordinary potential of 64 bits. In 1994, while Quentin Tarantino's masterpiece, *Pulp Fiction*, played in the movie theaters, Sony launched the PlayStation CD-ROM system. This was an enormous step forward in technology and graphics compared to competitors like the Nintendo 64 (1996), which still used cartridges.

Knowledgeable gamers had greater expectations and more requirements. Programmers aspired to create 3D games, and many pushed themselves to invent more complex scenarios and gameplay. This decade also saw a change in the tastes of adolescent gamers, who wanted to climb into the story and choose their own characters. New video game genres emerged, like the first-person shooter (FPS), of which *Wolfenstein 3D* (1992) was the prime example. *Monkey Island* (1990), one of the leading games for the Amiga 500 (1987), opened the way for a long tradition of graphic adventures, while *Mortal Kombat* (1992), with its movie-like realism, triggered the first controversies over violence in video games. One new genre engaged the most demanding gamers: real-time strategy (RTS), which borrowed concepts from the world of

board games. *Dune 2* (1992), based on Frank Herbert's science fiction novel *Dune*, was the first successful RTS game. In it, the player must create his own army and fight to conquer the planet, accumulating resources that allow him to construct buildings to strengthen his position. The virtual opponents change strategy based on a player's choices, making the game realistic and unpredictable.

The nineties were thus a period of rapid evolution in the gaming experience, thanks to technological leaps (in hardware and software, but above all in the global spread of the internet) as well as changes in consumer tastes and the cultural perception of video games.

THE 2000S
MULTIPLAYER GAMING

The worlds of movies and video games have grown ever closer. The cutscenes in video games have come to rival the silver screen. At the dawn of video gaming, social context influenced game themes. Today, it is video games that influence culture, inspire movies, and enter into the collective imagination. In the era of the 128-bit console, graphics have become ever more realistic, and thanks to the internet, gamers around the world can challenge each other online. Digital distribution platforms like Steam (2003) emerged, and *World of Warcraft* (2004) became the most widely played online game in the world, with more than five million subscribers. Even the colossus Microsoft entered the video game fray with the Xbox (2001), while Sony confirmed its leadership with the PlayStation 2 (2000). Nintendo answered with the GameCube (2000), abandoning cartridges for the mini-DVD. SEGA left the console market following the low sales of the Dreamcast, its last platform (1999). In 2004, Nintendo reinvented the portable console with the Nintendo DS, equipped with two screens, one of them a touchscreen.

Gameplay became ever more immersive, and thanks to artificial intelligence, video games became "open world," allowing characters to move freely, react independently to what was happening, and interact with the virtual environment. *Grand Theft Auto: San Andreas* (2004) is an example of what open world video games can offer. *Assassin's Creed* (2007) initiated a strong series of adventure video games that reconstructed various historical eras.

THE 2010S
INDIE VIDEO GAMES

Who would have thought that sales of video games would exceed those of movies and music together? By the 2010s, the video gaming industry was closing in on 120 billion dollars, as productions became ever more spectacular. But independent titles were also capturing market share. *Minecraft* (2009) may be the most famous indie video game, but *Cuphead* (2017), inspired by cartoons of the 1930s, has also achieved great success. The PlayStation 4 (2013) and the Xbox One (2013) were so close in performance that what made the difference were the exclusive games for each platform. These years saw the release of some of the most immersive games ever produced, including *Portal 2* (2011), *The Elder Scrolls V: Skyrim* (2013), *The Last of Us* (2013), *The Witcher 3* (2015), *The Legend of Zelda: Breath of the Wild* (2017)—and *Fortnite* (2017), which became a mass phenomenon. Identification with the gameplay and accurately rendered scenery and characters were now de rigueur, and competition among developers reached the highest level.

After the Wii U (2012) flopped, Nintendo tried to refine its idea of the hybrid console with the Switch (2017). But by now portability had become the prerogative of smartphones, and many titles were designed for these devices. The famous *Angry Birds* (2009) was a sort of gateway to gaming for casual players of all ages.

THE 2020S
HYPERREALISM + VR

Video games flourished during the pandemic, and, fittingly, the PlayStation 5 and the Xbox Series X, consoles with almost identical technical characteristics, both came out in late 2020. With 4K and modern graphics drivers, they achieved unimaginable levels of definition. The fidelity of the scenery, faces, and character movement in video games could now be defined as hyperrealism. In fact, today's video games have little to fear from the movies. Famous actors are lending their faces and voices to video game characters; for example, Keanu Reeves became Johnny Silverhand in *Cyberpunk 2077* (2020). Confirming the presence of video games in daily life are movies like *Sonic the Hedgehog* (2020), which brought the SEGA character to the big screen.

Sony spent a decade developing its PlayStation VR, and after years of experimenting with Oculus Rift, Mark Zuckerberg, the head of Meta, developed more powerful goggles (Oculus Quest 2) that immersed players completely in the game. Tactile sensors and other devices still under development will revolutionize the gaming experience again. The future of video games is still being written.

FOLLOWING PAGES: Boys playing *Enduro Racer* on an Atari ST in a computer store in 1989.

INTRODUCTION

FIRST GENERATION

FROM THE ARCADE TO THE LIVING ROOM

coin changes the world! The video game revolution exploded in the coin-operated arcades, where the sound of quarters dropping combined with repetitive electronic music encoded in just a few digital bits. The first game distributed on a large scale was *Pong* (1972), but arcades truly took off when intergalactic battles came to life on the little colored screens. As millions of kids crowded into the gaming halls, the concept of e-sports was born with the first recorded tournament, a *Spacewar!* contest at Stanford University in 1972. Magnavox launched the first TV console, the Odyssey, which Atari followed with a home version of *Pong*. The evolution of the little bouncing ball was just around the corner. *Breakout*, with its colored wall of little bricks, led the way to modern gameplay. And who can forget *Gran Trak 10*, *Speed Race*, and the first driving simulators? It's the seventies, baby, and the world is changing. . . .

TWENTIETH CENTURY-FOX Presents A LUCASFILM LTD. PRODUCTION STAR WARS
Starring MARK HAMILL HARRISON FORD CARRIE FISHER
PETER CUSHING
and
ALEC GUINNESS

Written and Directed by   Produced by   Music by
GEORGE LUCAS   GARY KURTZ   JOHN WILLIAMS

PANAVISION® PRINTS BY DE LUXE® TECHNICOLOR®

Making Films Sound Better

Original Motion Picture Soundtrack on 20th Century Records and Tapes

DOLBY SYSTEM®
Noise Reduction · High Fidelity

© 1977 20TH CENTURY-FOX

A NEW WAY TO PLAY

In a bar at the end of the street, a handful of kids gather around a strange cabinet with colored designs. One of them inserts a coin, then works a handle and some buttons with ever more emphasis, as if he were fighting a boxing match. New sounds fill the air, less mechanical than the ones from the pinball machine nearby, vaguely recalling missiles or cannon fire. The boys' faces are lit by a monitor, and their gazes are sucked into worlds in outer space, like those in the Star Wars saga, which has just begun thrilling millions worldwide with the episode *A New Hope* (1977). This is where the spread and success of video games begins.

The arcade cabinets, called coin-ops in the United States, forever changed the way kids play. The idea of moving spaceships or characters around on a screen was an exciting novelty, and it gave a satisfying feeling of control never felt before. Japan began to crank out animated cartoons about big robots like Jeeg, Mazinga, and Goldrake. Pink Floyd broke down the walls of social convention with their masterpiece *The Wall*, and American president Jimmy Carter soured relations with the Soviets by ordering a grain embargo. Perhaps no one at the time expected that electronic entertainment would become what it is today, but for many it only took a coin to escape reality and ignite a new passion.

In 1977, *A New Hope*, the first episode of the Star Wars saga, came out in theaters. It would change the worlds of both movies and video games.

THE GOLDEN AGE OF THE ARCADE CABINET

t first, arcade games were very physical. Most were played standing up, and, as with pinball, commands issued to the machine were often accompanied by whole-body movements. This did not necessarily improve performance or scoring, but it did confirm the player's identification with the experience. In 1972, *Pong* became the first true arcade video game sold on a large scale, with 19,000 units produced and distributed throughout the world. Created by the inventors of *Computer Space*, *Pong* reproduced electronically the classic game of ping-pong. Armed with loads of coins and patience, the kids of the seventies crowded into the bars and public places where arcade cabinets found ever more space.

However, as always happens with great revolutions in popular culture, criticism of video games was not far behind. Not so much about the subjects, which were still considered innocuous, but the level of kids' involvement with the games. The first parents' committees emerged, comparing video games to drugs and accusing them of distracting boys from their schoolwork. But when innovations this groundbreaking explode onto the scene, it is impossible to corral them. The golden age of the arcade cabinet brought a succession of popular titles to the gaming halls. Who doesn't remember *Space Invaders*, created by Tomohiro Nishikado and distributed by Taito in 1978? Or *Pac-Man*, created in 1980 by another Japanese programmer, Toru Iwatani, which made the fortunes of Bandai Namco and also helped define the history of the video game? Do you remember the first video game you played?

With its curved lines and a control panel inspired by Hollywood science fiction, the *Computer Space* cabinet still stands out today.

E-SPORTS
THE TOURNAMENTS BEGIN

The challenge is everything in video games. The first known video game tournament took place on October 19, 1972, at Stanford University and involved about twenty participants playing the game *Spacewar!* *Rolling Stone* magazine sponsored the event and offered a year's subscription to the magazine as first prize. A tournament on the national level would not be held until 1980, when more than 10,000 participants challenged each other at *Space Invaders* on the Atari 2600 console. The tournament unfolded in various rounds throughout the United States and lasted six months. It ended in the spring of 1981 with a national champion: a precocious seventeen-year-old programmer, Rebecca Heineman, who still has an active career in video games today.

Spring 1981. The final phase of the Space Invaders Championship, begun the year before, is held in New York.

ODYSSEY
THE FIRST CONSOLE

In the summer of 1966, while waiting for a friend outside the bus station in Manhattan, Ralph H. Baer was struck by an idea. Taking out the yellow lined pad he always carried, he outlined in four pages the specifications for a new invention. His boss at Sanders Associates, an American defense contractor developing electronic systems, was intrigued by the idea and offered him $2,500 to pursue it. In 1968, Baer created the first prototype, called the Brown Box. And in September 1972, the first true console to work with home TV sets came out in stores: the Odyssey by Magnavox. The console offered only one game, a digital tennis match, in several variants. Swapping out some printed circuit boards changed the arrangement of elements on the screen and the response to inputs. The Odyssey displayed three square points and a line of variable length on the black-and-white screen, with the behavior of the points depending on the game. The console did not produce sound and could not keep score. To make the game less boring, the package included twelve transparent plastic panels to be attached to the television screen. These re-created, however crudely, twenty-seven different scenarios, from soccer to skiing. The kids would input commands using strange boxes with two dials and a button. Those who bought the optional rifle could play variants like "Prehistoric Safari" or "Shooting Gallery." Kids' expectations of video games were certainly not high at the time, and even with all its technological limitations, the Odyssey offered hours of entertainment.

The Magnavox Odyssey, the first home console, went on sale in August 1972, three months before Atari's *Pong* console came out.

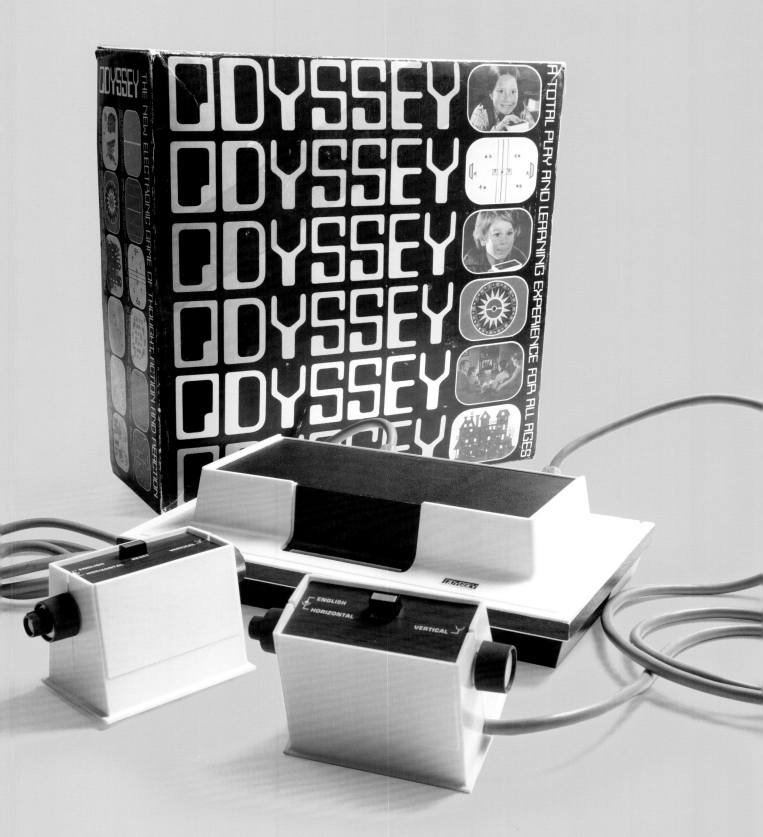

THE VIDEO GAMING INDUSTRY BEGINS

Thanks to the Odyssey, anyone could experience the thrill of the arcade in their living room. The console market had just opened up, and immediately the first legal skirmishes began. Magnavox accused Atari of plagiarizing the Odyssey with their game *Pong*, which came out a few months later. The case ended with a settlement. The Odyssey sold 100,000 units in the first year, but its price tag of $100 (more than $600 today) did not contribute to its success. In 1975, Atari produced its home version of *Pong*. In 1977, it was Nintendo's turn—well before the consoles we all know—with the *Color TV Game*, which came out in various versions, all still inspired by tennis. It is estimated that in those years, more than a thousand companies worldwide marketed consoles with some version of a tennis game.

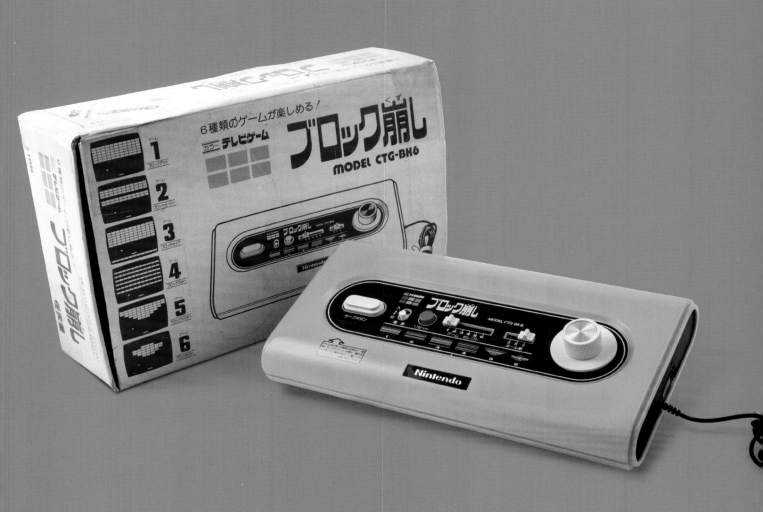

6種類のゲームが楽しめる！

カラー テレビゲーム

ブロック崩し

MODEL CTG-BK6

Nintendo

OPPOSITE: Atari's home console version of *Pong* (1975). During the Christmas shopping season that year, Atari sold 150,000 units.

ABOVE: Nintendo's *Color TV Game Block Kuzushi* (1979). Based on the game *Breakout*, it was designed by the legendary Shigeru Miyamoto.

ATARI
THE BIRTH
OF A DREAM

The home video game craze united children and parents in endless challenges in front of the TV set—at least at first. "Union" was also the meaning of the Greek word *syzygy* (συζυγία). In 1969, when California engineer Nolan Bushnell founded a company with his friend Ted Dabney, he wanted to call it "Syzygy," but this striking name was already in use. A fan of the Chinese board game Go, Bushnell settled on the term *atari*, a warning to a player that his opponent could take one of his pieces.

In 1972, the Bushnell's business took off in earnest. Atari Inc. would specialize in the design and construction of arcade cabinets, home consoles, home computers, and video games. The first employee Bushnell hired was Allan Alcorn, who would play a key role in the development of *Pong*. In May 1972, Bushnell was present for a demonstration of the Magnavox Odyssey, the first game console in history. He was so fascinated by the Odyssey that he asked Alcorn to create an arcade version of its tennis game.

Nolan Bushnell founded Atari in the early 1970s. The Sunnyvale company immediately specialized in designing and producing arcade cabinets, home consoles, and video games.

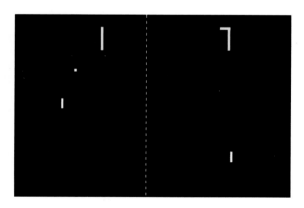

ABOVE: April 1971. The U.S. national table tennis team meets the Chinese team. This so-called "ping-pong diplomacy" improved relations between the two superpowers and facilitated the birth of *Pong*, the historic video game.

LEFT: A game of the arcade version of *Pong* (1972) in progress, score 1 to 7.

OPPOSITE: The *Pong* cabinet.

A REVOLUTION IN SIMPLICITY

On April 6, 1971, during the World Table Tennis Championships in Japan, the team from the People's Republic of China invited the U.S. team to China. A few days later, the U.S. team became the first Americans to set foot on Chinese territory since Mao Zedong and the Communist Party took power in 1949. The episode was called "ping-pong diplomacy." Table tennis gained a renewed interest among the young. That same year, Nolan Bushnell ordered a game simulating ping-pong from his employee Allan Alcorn. When Alcorn began working on the project, he did not know that his invention would change the way kids played forever. Bushnell couldn't have imagined it, either: for him, *Pong* (1972) was supposed to be a test. After three months of programming, Alcorn produced the electronic table tennis game that we all know. In the bar where the prototype was installed next to a *Computer Space* cabinet, a jukebox, and some pinball machines, it became the most popular coin-op game evening after evening. This success led Atari to expand its infrastructure and workforce to satisfy demand.

Some years later, in 1976, Bushnell decided to create a new video game. He entrusted the project to a stubborn young Californian who, a few years before, had planted himself in the Atari lobby, stalking Bushnell until he hired

him: Steve Jobs. For this new challenge, Jobs enlisted his friend Steve Wozniak, who was then employed at Hewlett Packard. The objective was to make the game work with fewer than fifty chips on the board. Wozniak worked day and night to complete the job, but Atari never used his final design, which was so cleverly optimized that the company would have had to retrain its technicians to understand its intricacies.

Instead, *Breakout* was released in 1976 with a board containing one hundred chips. The gameplay was more interesting than that of *Pong*, and the player could develop specific strategies to win more points. Shortly after *Breakout* was released, Jobs left Atari, along with Wozniak, to found the Apple Computer Company. Jobs offered Bushnell shares in the new company, but received a curt refusal. The guru of Atari already had everything he could want from life. . . .

After the sale of Atari, Nolan Bushnell (right) and Steve Wozniak (left) continued to collaborate, launching a new line of robotic stuffed toys, the Petsters, in 1985.

PONG VS. BREAKOUT

Table tennis is based on a very simple idea, even if the games can be extremely fierce. The elegant, intuitive gameplay of *Pong* centered on how the ball hit the "paddle": the farther it struck from the center of the little beam, the more inclined its trajectory. To keep the game from becoming too long and boring, the ball sped up after the fourth and twelfth volleys. These little tricks represented the first attempts to create a gaming experience that was more engaging and realistic.

From this simple idea, the new world of video gaming evolved. *Breakout* exemplified this evolution: it took the concept of *Pong* and innovated on the mechanics and gameplay. The player bounced the ball off the horizontal paddle to hit and destroy the wall of bricks above. Each row of bricks had a different color and point value; for example, the first row was yellow, and each brick was worth one point. Successive rows were worth more, but the ball sped up, increasing the difficulty. When the ball punched through the last row and touched the ceiling, the paddle automatically became half as long. A player had three rounds before the dreaded Game Over. The maximum score was 896, achieved by knocking down two entire screens of bricks.

Breakout became an iconic game, and it reappeared over the years in different forms, such as *Arkanoid* (1986), *Puchi Carat* (1997) and *Wizorb* (2011).

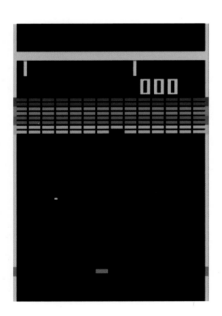

LEFT: The arcade version of *Breakout* (1976).

OPPOSITE: Promotional flyers for *Breakout* and a *Pong* clone, first to get them into bars, and then into gaming arcades.

CHICAGO COIN PRESENTS THE WINNER!

speedway

All the Fabulous Excitement of Actual Speedway Racing! Spectacular Realism! Breath-taking Action! Multiple Sound Effects and Color! 3-D Effect.

FOOL-PROOF, TROUBLE-FREE DESIGN
with Amazing New Full Color Projection Principle.

NO FILM! NO BELTS!
NO PHOTO-ELECTRIC CELL
that may give trouble.

REALISTIC DRIVING!
Player Controls an Actual Scale-Model Racing Car in Racing Competition with Other Cars! 6 competitor cars vary their speeds and positions on the track, creating spine-tingling speedway situations for the player . . . accidents—passing—lane hugging, etc.

And, to add to the exciting appeal—

REALISTIC RACE CAR SOUNDS
which are linked to the speed and the occurence of accidents.

Mfrs. of PROVEN PROFIT MAKERS Since 1931

CHICAGO COIN MACHINE DIV.
CHICAGO DYNAMIC INDUSTRIES, INC.
1725 W. DIVERSEY BLVD., CHICAGO, ILLINOIS 60614

See other side for further details.

A GAME THAT CAN TAKE A 25c COIN CHUTE!

THE FIRST DRIVING SIMULATORS

The fascination of video games lies in their potential to simulate reality. From the very first releases, driving games have always held a particular interest in this regard. At the end of the sixties, in the Salt Lake City amusement park where a young Nolan Bushnell earned his first money maintaining the electromechanical coin-op machines, the most played game was *Speedway* by Chicago Coin (1969). It was a kind of forerunner of electronic driving simulators: a reel of cars ran on the screen, and the player, using a mechanical steering wheel, tried to avoid crashing his own vehicle into them. When he founded Atari, Bushnell planned to develop a video game like *Speedway*, but in the end he opted for *Pong*.

The first electronic driving simulator had to await the release of the Magnavox Odyssey in 1972. The console included a game called *Wipeout*, in which the player moved a point of light around a racetrack outlined by a sheet laid over the television screen. The game also required the use of physical objects, such as a scoreboard, tokens, and pit stop cards. In 1973, Atari issued *Space Race*, an arcade game in which the players controlled spaceships engaged in fighting enemy ships and avoiding comets and meteors. It was designed for two players, with black-and-white graphics and controlled by a bidirectional joystick. The next year, Atari produced the first driving video game for arcades: *Gran Trak 10*, which presented a top-down view of a track in black and white. At the end of 1974, Taito issued *Speed Race*, created by Tomohiro Nishikado (who would design *Space Invaders* a few years later). In *Speed Race*, the first video game with vertical scrolling, the player drove in a straight line, avoiding other cars.

Electromechanical games like *Speedway* marked an era and prepared the way for arcade cabinets.

SECOND GENERATION

GENERATION

THE HEYDAY AND COLLAPSE OF THE VIDEO GAME INDUSTRY

1976-1982

ears of gold, years of lead. The end of the seventies and the beginning of the eighties witnessed the evolution of the video game, with historic titles, from *Space Invaders* to *Pac-Man*; new ways to play, from artistic arcade cabinets to the legendary Commodore 64; the dawn of miniaturization, with the portable Game & Watch series; and the race toward greater immersion, which was not always easy to achieve, as shown by *E.T.* ("the ugliest game of all time").

But these were also the years when families and institutions declared war on gaming. Brutal years, when even the giants could not break even. Atari's crisis led to the destruction of hundreds of thousands of cartridges, buried in the desert and uncovered thirty years later near the city of Alamogordo, New Mexico—the so-called "Pompeii of video games." This episode put an end to the heroic era of gaming and opened the door to the wind from the East.

SCORE 1   HI SCORE   SCORE 2
  0040   0000   0000

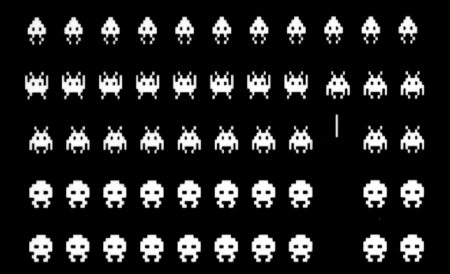

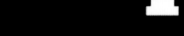

2 ⬆⬆   CREDIT 00

INVASION FROM OUTER SPACE

The year was 1978, and thirty-four-year-old Tomohiro Nishikado was programming his masterpiece, *Space Invaders*. These were the years of *Star Wars* (1977) and the space probe *Voyager*. For nine years, Nishikado had been working on electromechanical games at Taito Corporation of Tokyo. A talented engineer in the capital of video game innovation, he did not hesitate when he was asked to learn electronic arcade games. He had a vision: alien hordes descending from outer space to Earth, like an incessant rain. Having already drafted the idea in his electromechanical game *Space Monsters*, he realized it fully on the screen of an 8-bit system. Controlled by an Intel 8080 CPU, with sound effects from the Texas Instruments SN76477 audio processor, little monsters with antennae dropped down, loosing bombs on the earthlings. The player shot missiles up at them from a cannon that could only be maneuvered from side to side, and took shelter under defensive bunkers. As the aliens were eliminated, the rhythm of their descent sped up. Thus, the difficulty and tension increased, matched by the ever more frenetic background music. Once the player was hit three times, the game would end. Simple concepts that created an enthralling game, and would serve as the basis for many games to come.

OPPOSITE: The first arcade version of *Space Invaders* (1978) was in black and white. Color effects were simulated by green and orange films applied to the glass.

RIGHT: The Atari 2600 version (1980) added color.

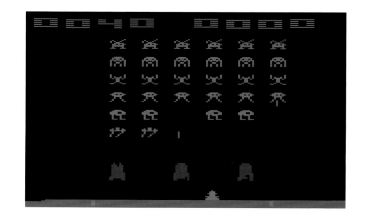

Space Invaders soon became a worldwide success. It had as much impact on popular culture as the Beatles; the *New York Times* described the craze for the game as "the great Space Invaders invasion of 1979." The *Space Invaders* boom also shook public opinion. Associations of parents and some local governments attacked video games, accusing them of fomenting turbulence and distraction in the "fragile" minds of children. The city of Mesquite, Texas, forbade those under seventeen to play video games unsupervised in public, prompting a swift reaction from one chain of arcades, which asserted children's "right to socialize." The case reached the Supreme Court, and the ordinance was annulled. Japan also tried unsuccessfully to ban the game, claiming that it instigated truancy. Some physicians joined the crusade against *Space Invaders*, diagnosing a new pathology in those who played too much: "*Space Invaders* elbow."

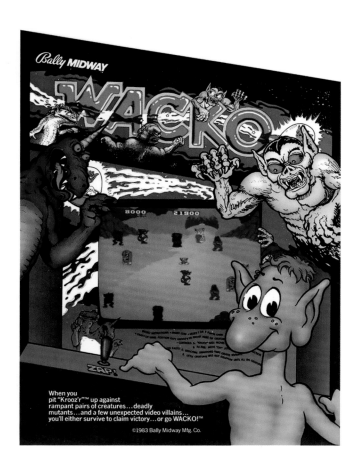

THE IMPORTANCE OF IMMERSION

What drew millions of kids to the arcades was an irresistible mix of novelty and immersion. Video games were clearly the new face of the gaming world, and the design of the arcade cabinets themselves played an important role. It wasn't enough to provide a box with a monitor and buttons. In many cases the arcade cabinet was specifically designed to make the gaming experience as engaging and realistic as possible. For example, some cutting-edge cabinets came equipped with cockpits for race car drivers or spaceship pilots.

The very first cabinets, like *Space Invaders* (1978), already contained the seeds of this trend. The design of the Taito cabinet, licensed in the U.S. to Midway Games, is typical: the minimal graphics of the video game were elevated by their innovative and attractive packaging. The video game was not displayed directly on a cathode ray tube monitor, but projected from the CRT through a set of mirrors to a sheet of glass with a desolate planet drawn on the back. A bezel (screen shield) with border designs replicating the style of the background complemented the scene. These three levels of graphics, one digital and two analog, gave the player a more immersive experience than earlier cabinets.

In 1983, Midway created *Wacko*, in which the entire arcade cabinet was slanted. The board also featured innovative controls: two joysticks and a central trackball. Players took the role of Kapt'n Krooz'r, a small green alien who commanded a spaceship. To advance, they had to eliminate all the monsters on each level: blue lizard-men, black-clad space vampires, two-headed yellow dragons, brown mud men, and red monsters. The gameplay was made more complex by the inclined cabinet and the unusual controls. The central trackball moved the spaceship, while the left and right joysticks fired the weapons. This original design made the gaming experience more engaging than the typical buttons.

The *Wacko* cabinet, with its tilted control board, reflected the need to impress demanding gamers with the hardware as well as the software.

FAIRCHILD CHANNEL F VS. ATARI 2600
ENTERTAINMENT IN A CARTRIDGE

By now, the dream of playing video games at home on the TV had come true for many kids. After the initial enthusiasm, however, interest in the first consoles dropped off, due to the lack of variety on the market. In fact, the only video game available within the walls of the home was ping-pong, albeit in a dozen variants. It would be normal for boredom to set in after many rounds. So how could the passion for video games be sustained? By creating new consoles, each with a different game, like the arcade cabinets? No, that would be too expensive for the public and risky for the developers. In 1976, the electronic engineer Jerry Lawson found the right solution: a CPU capable of reading video games stored on cartridges. Even if the graphics were still rudimentary and the RAM was limited to 64 bytes, a new revolution had begun. This first system was the VES, or Video Entertainment System (1976), soon rebranded as the Fairchild Channel F. The next year, Atari produced its first console with interchangeable cartridges, the VCS (Video Computer System), immediately renamed the Atari 2600 (1977). More powerful than the Fairchild Channel F and with greater resources for marketing and development, the Atari platform sold some 30 million units and is still an icon to all video game enthusiasts. Nolan Bushnell's idea was to bring home the experience of the games that were already successful in the arcades and amplify it with new titles. In 1980, the company also put the Atari 400 and the Atari 800 on the market. These were home computers designed to conquer the market segment dominated by Commodore and Apple, and they too sold very well.

ABOVE: The iconic Atari CX40 joystick, which became a symbol for an entire generation, thanks to its eight-way stick and the famous red button.

ABOVE: The first game cartridge for the Fairchild Channel F. It contained four very simple games, including tic-tac-toe, a screenshot from which is shown. The instructions were written on the cartridge.

FOLLOWING PAGES: The Fairchild Channel F next to the Atari 2600, also called the "Woody" because of its briar trim.

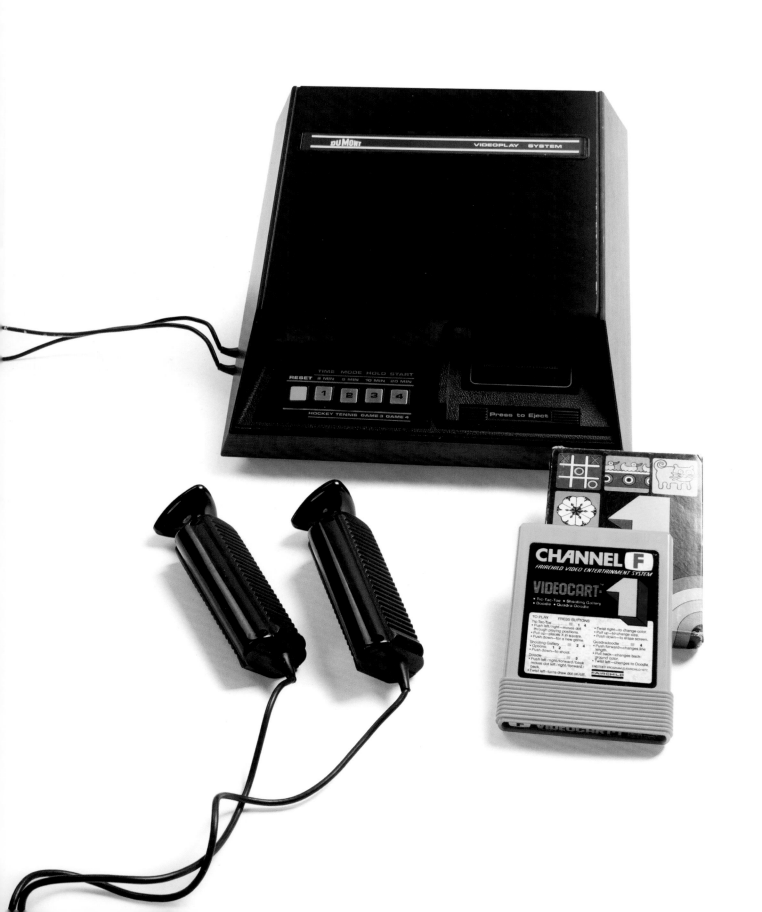

MB Microvision (1979), the first portable console, featured twelve interchangeable cartridges, each with its own processor and LCD screen.

MICROVISION AND GAME + WATCH
VIDEO GAMES IN YOUR POCKET

In 1979, portability became the watchword for the entire tech industry. In that year, Sony invented the Walkman, the revolutionary portable cassette player, and the Japanese phone company, NTT, launched the first commercial cell phone network. By now, video games had already entered homes in the form of consoles. The next step was to make these devices pocket-sized, too.

One of the first companies to try this was Nintendo, which in 1980 created its famous Game & Watch. This line of elementary video games used a little monochrome LCD screen, similar to those found on digital wristwatches. Gameplay was limited to moving characters around on the screen and finding the proper timing for their predetermined actions. In *Fire* (1980), the object of the game was to make the people jumping from a burning building land on a tarp so they could be taken safely to an ambulance. The challenge was coordinating the leaps of all the people who emerged from the building one after another. Other companies, like Epoch, Coleco, and Nintendo itself, then created mini arcade cabinets, called "tabletops." These imitated the shape, artwork, and of course the names of the best-known arcade games, but had many limitations compared to the originals, including inferior graphics. Notwithstanding their success, which lasted to the end of the eighties, the tabletops could not be considered true consoles, because they could not be programmed. Back in 1979, Milton Bradley Company—the famous MB, the American producer of board games and toys—had already created Microvision, a portable video game device with interchangeable cartridges. Thanks to these two characteristics, portability and the ability to play multiple games on the same device, the Microvision is considered the first true handheld console. Unfortunately, this initial experiment did not have much success, because of the small size of the screen and the limited portfolio of games: only twelve titles.

FOLLOWING PAGES: From left, the classic Game Boy (1989); the *Vermin* Game & Watch (1980); the Micro Vs. System (1984); the Atari Touch Me (1979); the SEGA Game Gear (1991); and the tabletop *Mario's Cement Factory*, a spinoff of *Mario Bros*.

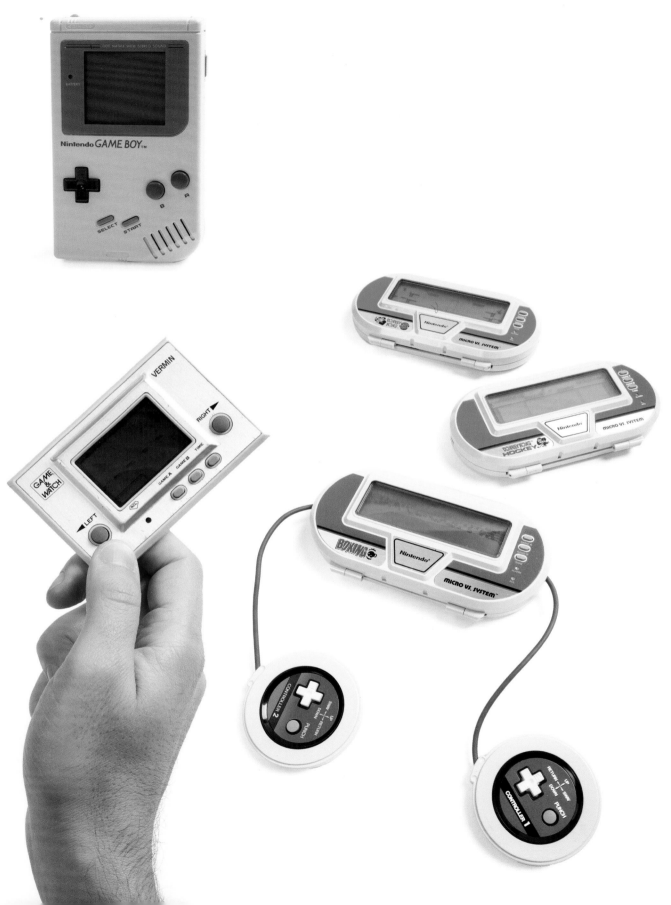

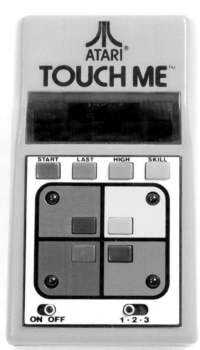

PAC-MAN
A TIMELESS CLASSIC

If you were asked, "What's the most famous video game of all time?" what would you say? Surely many people would answer *Pac-Man*, because of the hold that this simple and immediate game still has on the popular imagination. This classic has endured because anyone can try it out without any special skill. And after you've played it once, you immediately want to play it again.

For the few who don't know *Pac-Man*, the purpose of the game is to guide a friendly, big-mouthed yellow creature as it eats all the dots that line a maze of meandering paths. Pac-Man's enemies are four ghosts who also wander the maze. After swallowing one of the special pills at the corners of the screen, Pac-Man can temporarily eat the ghosts; otherwise, he is forced to flee them. To complicate things, each ghost has its own characteristics. Blinky, red, is the most aggressive, and tends to follow Pac-Man. Pinky, pink, is less aggressive, but faster. Inky, blue, is smarter, and tries to block the tunnel nearest Pac-Man. Finally, Clyde, orange, is considered the stupidest of the four ghosts, because it wanders around aimlessly and is also the slowest.

IT ALL STARTED WITH A PIZZA

T wo anecdotes about the most famous game in the world. First: Toru Iwatani, the father of *Pac-Man*, has said that a pizza with a missing slice, encountered at a dinner with friends, is what inspired him to create his unforgettable character. Second: although the game was designed never to run out of levels, a programming bug at level 256 caused half the game screen to display incorrectly, making it impossible to get to the next level.

Pac-Man was everywhere in the eighties. Here, the sheriff of Dinosaur, Colorado, plays his favorite video game, *Ms. Pac-Man*, in his wife's bar.

COMMODORE
NOT JUST
VIDEO GAMES

In 1977, the American company Commodore released the PET, one of the first 8-bit computers. Four years later, they put out a more compact and affordable model, the VIC 20, which hastened the spread of personal computers as well as video gaming. Equipped with this device (which included a built-in keyboard), a screen, and a BASIC language manual, anyone could write their own programs. Or they could play preprogrammed games loaded from cartridges—as on the Atari 2600 and other consoles—or from tapes or floppy disks. Video gaming with the VIC 20 and particularly with its greatly improved successor, the Commodore 64 (1982), meant having a vast array of titles available, and the power of the new microprocessors in these computers raised the bar for the gaming experience. The graphics, animation, and music exceeded the quality of the home consoles of the era. One could say that, from this moment, video gamers split into two camps: the supporters of personal computers and the supporters of consoles.

A Commodore 64 with a Datassette reader and a 5.25-inch floppy disk drive. *Out Run* was one of the most iconic driving games of the era.

FORBIDDEN FOREST ON THE C64

Notwithstanding the tedium of loading video games from Datassettes or the risk of damaging fragile 5.25-inch floppy disks, the capabilities of the C64 shone with titles like *Forbidden Forest* (1983). Technically advanced for the era, with enormous sprites and animations never seen before, this title offered gameplay that was neither simple nor banal. Armed with a bow and arrows, the protagonist must survive the monsters he encounters in the forest, including giant spiders and flying insects. The game's sound was also cutting-edge, thanks to the C64's excellent audio chip.

E.T. THE EXTRA-TERRESTRIAL
THE UGLIEST GAME OF ALL TIME

The term "gaming experience" refers to everything that allows players to immerse themselves in a game as if it were real life. Of course, early video game technology did not allow for the level of immersion that we enjoy in today's most ambitious games. But games licensed from movies still exerted a powerful attraction. It was exciting for a kid in the eighties to take on the role of a big-screen hero.

However, when the all-important immersion is not achieved, a video game's failure is guaranteed. A case in point was *E.T. the Extra-Terrestrial* (1982), inspired by the blockbuster film by Steven Spielberg. Atari did not want to miss the opportunity to develop a video game that built on the popularity of the endearing alien with the glowing finger. For this task, Atari called on Howard Scott Warshaw, an Atari programmer who had already designed famous games like *Yar's Revenge* (1981) and *Raiders of the Lost Ark* (1982), inspired by the Indiana Jones movie.

Warshaw was given just five weeks to create the game, so that it could be on store shelves in time for Christmas—and, as is often the case, haste did nothing for quality. Instead of opting for a simple and safe solution with a video game in the *Pac-Man* style, Warshaw tried a more original idea. In fact, he wanted to develop a game based on the story of the movie, in hopes of re-creating the emotional experience of watching it. However, he could not bring all his ideas to fruition in such a short time. The result not only disappointed kids' hopes for an *E.T.* game but also created a general sense of disillusionment that led to the 1983 crisis in the American video game market.

The Atari 2600 cartridge for *E.T. the Extra-Terrestrial* (1982). The game's designer, Howard Scott Warshaw, went on to work on another title, *Saboteur*, in hopes of salvaging Atari's financial situation, but it was never released.

REDEMPTION AFTER FORTY YEARS

Even today, many puzzle over the decisions that went into designing what has become known as the ugliest video game of all time. However, forty years on, this reputation has actually made *E.T. the Extra-Terrestrial* a coveted collector's item. In 2020, a sealed copy of the game sold on eBay for more than $1,000.

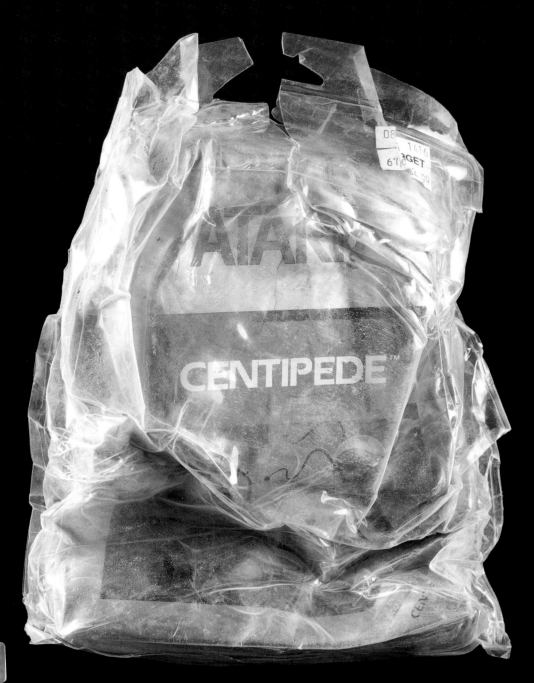

ALAMOGORDO
THE POMPEII OF VIDEO GAMES

Unfortunately, the fabled Atari was not immune to commercial shocks, and in 1983, the crisis in the video game market led the firm into decline. The immediate crisis was the flop of *E.T. the Extra-Terrestrial*, but the underlying cause was the saturation of the market with so many video games—often underwhelming ports of arcade titles—that did not meet kids' expectations. Numerous retailers returned unsold inventory and asked for refunds, and Atari ended up dumping hundreds of thousands of overstock cartridges in the city landfill of Alamogordo, New Mexico. The 2014 excavation of buried video games from the landfill was recounted in the documentary *Atari: Game Over*, directed by Zak Penn. This excavation is recognized as the first example of video game archeology, and many of the items retrieved were sold for dizzying prices on the Internet.

An original copy of *Centipede*, one of the 1,300 video game cartridges recovered in the dig at Alamogordo in 2014.

THIRD GENERATION

8-BITS AND THE FAR EAST

1983–1990

In the eighties, the triumph of the Land of the Rising Sun was as resounding as the repetitive notes of *Donkey Kong*—the game that introduced Mario, the mustachioed plumber who would take Nintendo to the top with his spinoff, *Super Mario Bros*. This era saw the birth of the Game Boy, and the genius of three Japanese engineers who changed the gaming experience: Hideo Kojima, Shigeru Miyamoto, and Yu Suzuki, who created titles like *Metal Gear*, *Zelda*, and *Out Run*, with hidden bonuses, realistic graphics, and three-dimensional animation. Their fertile creativity launched the first real console war among the giants of the market, Nintendo and SEGA. While the joystick slowly transformed into the joypad, giving the player more freedom and comfort, a young unknown behind the Iron Curtain, Alexey Pajitnov, created the first puzzle game in history—*Tetris*, which would become a global success.

JAPAN'S RISE BEGINS

The 1983 crisis in the North American video game industry gave Japan an opportunity to introduce a new way of gaming to the international market. While Michael Jackson sent three singles from his album *Thriller* to the top of the charts, kids in the Land of the Rising Sun got to know the Nintendo Family Computer (1983), also known by the abbreviation Famicom, a new 8-bit console that revolutionized the playing experience. For the modest sum of 14,800 yen (about $350 today), kids could finally play *Donkey Kong*, *Donkey Kong Jr.*, and *Popeye* in versions very similar to those in the arcades. Nintendo had succeeded where Atari failed: in re-creating the arcade experience at home. As a result, the sales potential—and entertainment value—of video games was drastically increased. The success of the Famicom spread worldwide, and in 1985, the console reached the United States, with a new design and a new name: the Nintendo Entertainment System, better known as the NES.

The Nintendo Family Computer, the first cartridge console from the Japanese colossus. The console boasted many accessories, including a keyboard, a floppy drive, a robot, and a pair of 3D glasses for virtual reality.

A GREATER FREEDOM OF MOVEMENT

The first game controllers consisted of a small wheel that communicated elementary movements, as in *Pong* (1972). In 1976, for his Fairchild Channel F, Jerry Lawson transformed the controller into a rudimentary joystick without a base, held in the hand and manipulated with the thumb. On top was a sort of cap for directional control. The true joystick came out the following year, when Atari paired its VCS with the CX40, the iconic black joystick with a single red button. Thanks to its flat base, the player could

place it on a surface. Fluid movement was unfortunately still far off, and wrists could be sorely tested during long gaming sessions. In 1978, Atari tried again with its Trackball: a ball set into a base, which allowed 360 degrees of movement, compared to the eight directions allowed by the classic joystick.

The Famicom/NES (1983) introduced a new type of controller that was much more light, precise, and maneuverable: the gamepad (or joypad). The directional cross was the idea of the brilliant Gunpei Yokoi (1941-1997), one of Nintendo's most prolific inventors. To him we also owe Game & Watch (1980-1991) and the Game Boy (1989), as well as various video games. Freedom of movement was no longer a problem, and fatigue was only a memory. Game developers also saw the potential of the new controllers; they created sequences of directional movements and button presses that triggered special moves, like those in fighting games. The directional cross was so effective that, all these years later, we still find it on the controllers for all the latest consoles.

The Nintendo Entertainment System, better known as the NES. Sales reached about 62 million units.

1983-1990

DRAGON'S LAIR
EXTREME VISUAL IMPACT

In the first episode of the second season of the TV series *Stranger Things*, the young protagonists gather in an arcade, in front of a very specific game: *Dragon's Lair* (1983). At the beginning of the eighties, one of the principal limitations of video games was the graphics. The company Cinematronics decided to try a cutting-edge technology using laser discs. The famous animator Don Bluth was enlisted to work on the graphics, while Starcom and Advanced Microcomputer Systems concentrated on the programming side. This ambitious project aimed to transform an animated cartoon into a video game. The result was *Dragon's Lair*, in which the knight Dirk the Daring strove to save the beautiful princess Daphne from the terrible dragon Singe.

From a visual point of view, the game was extraordinary, but players had very little freedom of action. They could only make instantaneous joystick movements or press a button to use Dirk's sword. If the player took the correct action, the story continued, and the next scene of the film was shown. Otherwise, a death sequence was displayed. Unfortunately, it wasn't always clear which action was needed, so the player had to proceed by trial and error. But there were some forty different scenes and more than 600 different moves to be properly executed. Due to these limitations and its cost (two or three coins per game), *Dragon's Lair* was soon labeled a money-eater. However, the cabinet had another innovative characteristic: a second, upper screen, where the next player could follow the game or simply enjoy the beautiful animations.

TOP: The 3DO version of *Dragon's Lair* (1994), one of the most faithful ports of the original videodisc, which came out in 1983. The game offered different death sequences depending on the wrong action taken.

BOTTOM: A screenshot from the original videodisc version (1983).

TETRIS
FROM RUSSIA WITH INTERLOCKING

In 1984, when the Iron Curtain was still some way from falling, a young engineer named Alexey Pajitnov was a researcher at the Academy of Sciences in Moscow. To test the power of an Elektronika 60 computer, he created a pastime that would go down in history: *Tetris*, the first puzzle game. It is a video game of logic and reasoning, in which geometric shapes drop randomly from the top of the screen and must be joined together so as not to leave empty spaces. *Tetris* creates a truly addictive gaming experience: as soon as players finish a game, they start a new one to try to beat their own score. (An ideal for all video game developers.) *Tetris*'s unique combination of simplicity and skill ensured its immediate success and its status as one of the greatest games of all time. When Pajitnov showed his colleagues his invention, he was not aware of its potential economic value. But within a few days, *Tetris* was already installed on half the computers in Moscow. Ironically, during the Cold War, it was an American firm that developed the commercial potential of *Tetris*, through a licensing deal with the Soviet state.

After its spread began in the mid-eighties, *Tetris* achieved its greatest success in 1989, with the Game Boy version by Nintendo.

Nintendo GAME BOY™

DMG-TR-EUR

MADE IN JAPAN
FABRIQUE AU JAPON

TETRIS™*

ORIGINAL
GAME LINK
GAME PAK

Nintendo

Original
Nintendo
Seal of
Quality

THIS SIDE OUT CE COTE A L'EXTERIEUR
HERAUSRAGENDE SEITE

THE MEN WHO REINVENTED GAMING

The Nintendo Game Boy in its original white version, with some of its best-known games.

GUNPEI YOKOI

Ironically, sometimes it is boredom that leads to a breakthrough insight. This was true for Gunpei Yokoi, one of Nintendo's first video game developers. At the end of the seventies, Yokoi saw a businessman on the train pressing the buttons on his LCD calculator for no apparent reason other than to pass the time. This encounter gave rise to the idea that became the Game & Watch. Those who lived through the eighties will remember how much these electronic gadgets defined that decade. To have *Donkey Kong* or *Popeye* or another famous game in your pocket (even in a much more limited version than the original) was a prospect irresistible to many kids. Starting in 1980, Gunpei Yokoi developed the the Game & Watch for a full decade, updating the design of the devices, adding a color LCD screen and backlighting, and enlarging the list of games with ports of ever more famous titles, from *Super Mario Bros.* to *Zelda*. Then, in 1989, Yokoi changed pocket video games forever with the Game Boy, a console with interchangeable cartridges that you could carry everywhere. This was a revolutionary advance, particularly because many of the available titles were truly equivalent to the home console versions.

1983—1990

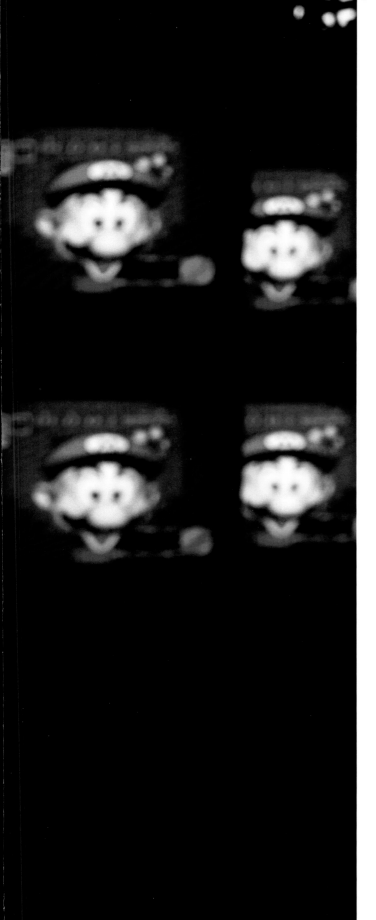

SHIGERU MIYAMOTO

Gunpei Yokoi was the man with the hardware ideas, but he was not solely responsible for the evolution of gameplay. In 1981, a young Shigeru Miyamoto was entrusted with the development of *Donkey Kong*, supervised by Yokoi. Over time, the ideas of the two men merged, producing extraordinary titles that defined the course of video game history: for example, *Mario Bros.* (1983) and *The Legend of Zelda* (1986), whose spinoffs have sold millions of copies worldwide. Miyamoto's game portfolio is vast, and marked by a particular talent for narrative. *Zelda* was an extremely engaging interactive story, one that created an imaginary realm of the sort hitherto found only in movies or books. Its success was aided by graphics with captivating colors, a game map planned to the slightest detail, and character design reminiscent of manga.

Shigeru Miyamoto is the father of Mario, who started as a character in *Donkey Kong* originally called Jumpman and was successfully spun off in 1983.

1983—1990

HIDEO KOJIMA

Hideo Kojima started out in the early 1980s as a young man who loved movies and video games. The futuristic and postapocalyptic worlds of *Blade Runner* (1982), *Terminator* (1984), and *Mad Max* (1985) inspired him to create *Metal Gear* (1987), which first came out for the MSX home computer and then was ported to the NES and other platforms. The main character, Solid Snake, was catapulted into an enemy camp with minimal defensive gear. His goal was to recover munitions and escape unseen. *Metal Gear* was one of the first titles in the stealth genre, in which the character must survive various obstacles without attracting the attention of the enemy, controlled by the computer. The *Metal Gear* saga remains the most famous of its kind, and it continues to thrill with each new installment. Kojima has never stopped combining the worlds of movies and video games: titles like *Snatcher* (1988), *Policenauts* (1994), *Silent Hill* (1999), and *Death Stranding* (2019) have cemented his status as one of the most innovative game designers on the international stage.

OPPOSITE: Hideo Kojima with a life-size action figure of Sam Porter Bridges, the protagonist of his game *Death Stranding*, played by the actor Norman Reedus.

RIGHT: The NES version of *Metal Gear* (1987).

OUT RUN
THE BEST-LOVED DRIVING GAME OF ALL TIME

A group of drivers who are all a little bit nuts decide to enter a secret race across the United States, from New York to Los Angeles. Each driver has a different car, from a Lamborghini to a Rolls Royce to an ambulance. This is the storyline of the movie *The Cannonball Run* (1981), and in 1986, Yu Suzuku, a designer for SEGA, conceived of a video game that would reproduce the sensations of the crazy races in the movie. Having collected the necessary information on the landscapes and the cars, especially the Ferrari Testarossa convertible driven by the player, Suzuki brought forth *Out Run*. A timeless classic, this game contributed several innovations to the driving genre: the perspective from behind the car, which involved the player more; the duration of the game being extended not by staying on the track but by reaching checkpoints on time; and the ability (while driving up to 180 miles per hour) to choose between two roads, which changed the course of the game. The player could even choose which song to listen to during the drive, by setting the car radio at the beginning of the game. There were three available songs ("Magical Sound Shower," "Passing Breeze," and "Splash Wave"), plus a fourth ("Last Wave") that played at the end of the game. The three-dimensional animation relied on a modified version of the graphics driver from *Space Harrier* (1985), and the level of detail and fluidity was stunning. Throw in the fact that the game cabinet was shaped like a Ferrari Testarossa and simulated the vibrations of the road, and it's clear why *Out Run* was such a hit.

Inspired by the movie *The Cannonball Run* (1981), *Out Run* (1986) is still one of the most-played arcade games.

Some of the most famous video games for the SEGA Master System. Besides cartridges, the system also used SEGA cards, a more compact memory format similar to the HuCard in the NEC PC Engine, sold in North America as TurboGrafx-16.

NINTENDO VS. SEGA
THE FIRST REAL CONSOLE WAR

The marketplace is ruthless. As soon as Nintendo became the world leader in video games, other manufacturers tried to horn in—among them, SEGA. In 1983, while Nintendo was bringing the Family Computer onto the market, SEGA answered with its first console: the SG-1000. Hampered by its uncatchy name and an unimpressive list of titles, it had only limited success. The next year, SEGA tried again with an improved and more powerful model: the SG-1000 II or Mark II. But it was with their third attempt, the Mark III, known outside Japan as the SEGA Master System, that the competition really took off. Eight bits of computing power, if taken full advantage of, could yield very impressive games. With parts of the market still unexplored, it was possible to invent original genres, innovative ways of playing, and characters that would be stamped on the collective imagination forever, like Mario and Sonic the Hedgehog. Nintendo and SEGA targeted the so-called casual gamers, creating titles that offered gameplay more like the arcades and could engage those who might not be devoted players.

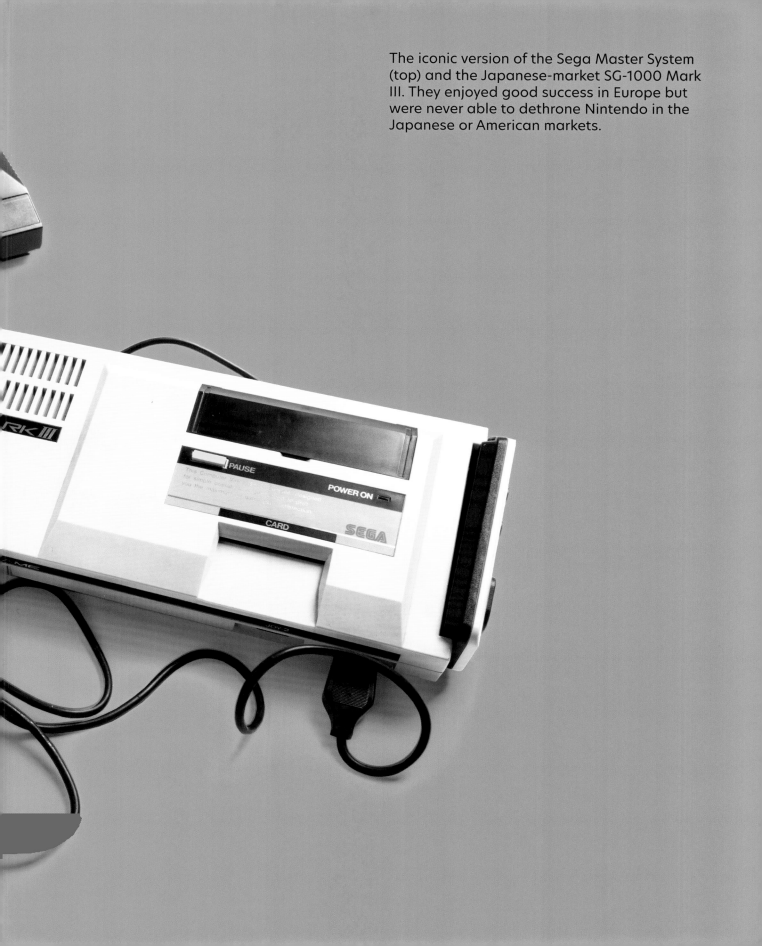

The iconic version of the Sega Master System (top) and the Japanese-market SG-1000 Mark III. They enjoyed good success in Europe but were never able to dethrone Nintendo in the Japanese or American markets.

NINTENDO
FROM PLAYING CARDS TO VIDEO GAMES

Charlie Chaplin said, "It is not reality that matters in a film but what the imagination can make of it." This saying can easily be applied to video games as well. Chaplin was born in 1889, the year Yamauchi Fusajiro founded Nintendo in Japan. Originally the famous video game manufacturer made and distributed playing cards, with a focus on *hanafuda* (flower cards), which could be used for various games. In the 1960s, when the playing card industry was in decline, Nintendo attempted to diversify, launching a taxi company, a chain of love hotels, a TV station, and a home appliance business. At the end of the sixties, the firm also began producing toys. Then, in the seventies, Nintendo released their first video game consoles, the Color TV Game series, inspired by *Pong*, *Breakout*, and *Speed Race*. The rest is history.

Hanafuda playing cards from the late fifties. The *hanafuda* deck is used to play different games, including *koi-koi*.

1983–1990

A collection of traditional Nintendo games, from a periscope and a "love tester" to a portable roulette wheel and a soccer board game.

6 8 BEAT **20** 15 POINTS **10 9**

HOUSE | DRAW | DRAW

GUM

BLACK JACK INSTRUCTIONS

- THE OBJECT OF THIS GAME IS TO BEAT THE "HOUSE" NUMBER ON THE CENTER REEL, YET NOT HAVE MORE THAN A TOTAL OF 21.
- AFTER OPENING SHUTTER OVER "HOUSE" NUMBER, NO MORE DRAWS CAN BE MADE.
- PLAYER MUST ALWAYS BEAT THE "HOUSE" NUMBER.
- 21 CAN ONLY BE BEATEN BY A BLACK JACK HAND WHICH IS MADE WHEN A "BLANK" APPEARS IN THE FIRST WINDOW, A "10" IN THE SECOND, AND AN "11" IN THE THIRD.
- ALL ODDS ARE INDICATED ON "HOUSE" WINDOW.

SEGA
FROM SLOT MACHINES TO ARCADE CABINETS

Standard Games (later, Service Games) was founded in Honolulu in 1940. Originally it imported jukeboxes and coin-op machines from the mainland U.S. to entertain the servicemen on the naval base at Pearl Harbor. In 1952, when the United States outlawed slot machines, the company began supplying the American bases in Japan instead; shortly thereafter, it began abbreviating SErvice GAmes to SEGA. In 1965, SEGA acquired a competing firm started by former U.S. Air Force officer David Rosen, and Rosen became the CEO of SEGA. Under his leadership, SEGA released its first electromechanical arcade game, *Periscope*, in 1966, the first step toward the arcade cabinets and consoles that we all know.

A SEGA Black Jack tabletop slot machine, one of the firm's coin-operated amusements for the American bases in Japan.

1983–1990

THE PLUMBER WHO REVOLUTIONIZED GAMING

In 1981, Nintendo leased a warehouse in Seattle to work on the American release of *Donkey Kong*. At the time, the Japanese company was not swimming in cash and even had trouble paying the rent. The owner of the warehouse, one Mario Segale, was very angry about the delay, but after a discussion with the American manager of Nintendo, he granted them a small extension. After this episode, the protagonist of *Donkey Kong*, previously called Jumpman, took on the name Mario. This character has since become the symbol of Nintendo and has generated head-spinning revenues, both from the many video game titles dedicated to him and from merchandise bearing his name.

But what was the secret of Mario's success? In terms of gameplay, his first and most noteworthy characteristic was how he jumped to avoid the barrels thrown by Donkey Kong in that famous platform game. The same ability featured in the first game entitled *Mario Bros.*, which came out in arcades in 1983. Alongside his brother Luigi, Mario must eliminate all the turtles and crabs that appear in each level, while avoiding fireballs and other obstacles.

But the real breakthrough came with *Super Mario Bros.* (1985), an expanded version of the original title. In this side-scrolling platform game, Mario must face turtles and other enemies to reach Bowser, the final boss, and free Princess Peach from his clutches. The gaming experience was enriched by many new elements. Hidden bonuses augmented Mario's abilities, making him bigger and stronger, increasing the height of his jump, or allowing him to shoot fireballs. There were also hidden levels and captivating music and sound effects, which made the game a perfect adventure for a home console, even if it was too long to adapt for the arcades. Between the original series and its spinoffs, Mario has sold more than 850 million copies to date.

The *Super Mario Bros* cartridge for the Italian market, distributed by Mattel. Today it has become a cult object for collectors and video game fans.

FOURTH GENERATION

MORE
DETAILED
AND
REALISTIC
ANIMATION

1987–1996

"Haven't you finished *Zelda* yet?" In the late 1980s, Nintendo anticipated YouTube gaming tutorials and offered the Nintendo Game Play telephone hotline and *Nintendo Power* magazine. Even the most difficult video games no longer had secrets. While the PC Engine showed the way to graphics superpower and the Amiga 500 found its way into countless homes, *Wolfenstein 3D* invented the first-person shooter, Blizzard Entertainment of *Warcraft* fame was born, and SEGA presented Sonic, the most famous mascot in the world. The increased computing power of PCs led to the still-unresolved question: which was better, the mouse or the controller? Two responses to the demand for immersion came from the Neo Geo super-cabinet and the Ferrari of consoles: Neo Geo AES. Meanwhile, Nintendo missed a historic opportunity to create the PlayStation, leaving it to Sony, and a new, fascinatingly unpredictable game experience appeared on the horizon: *SimCity*.

PC ENGINE
THE LITTLE CONSOLE WITH A BIG HEART

If you were to ask even the most jaded Japanese video gamer which console was most loved in the eighties, he would certainly say the PC Engine. This NEC console came out in 1987, during the reign of Nintendo and SEGA. The PC Engine boasted an 8-bit CPU and a 16-bit graphics coprocessor, placing it technologically halfway between the third and fourth generation of consoles. Its small size and satisfying ports of arcade titles assured its success. The games came on a new medium called the HuCard, a cartridge as big as a credit card but slightly thicker. The graphics power stunned the kids of the day, who could finally play with more detailed characters on their home TV sets and carry the console in their backpacks to their friends' houses. Playing titles like *Splatterhouse* (1988), one of the first side-scrolling fighting games

in the horror genre, was an exciting experience. The fluidity of the gameplay matched that of the arcade version. *Bonk's Adventure* (1990) was another successful title. The protagonist of this attractive platformer, a little caveman with a giant head, became the mascot of PC Engine as Mario did for Nintendo. His special moves—like the earthquake head knock, the head butt, and head strikes to deflect projectiles—gave him a unique playability and a charisma tinged with humor. With more than 1.5 million units sold in 1990, PC Engine captured 50 percent of the Japanese market. However, in the rest of the world, few appreciated this console's true capabilities, even when it was exported under the flashier name TurboGrafx-16. It would, in any case, remain a sort of status symbol for young Japanese gamers.

OPPOSITE: NEC's PC Engine (1987) enjoyed great success in Japan and had a library of almost nine hundred titles. In North America and Europe, the console was sold under the name TurboGrafx-16.

PRECEDING PAGES: The Super Nintendo controller (left) had the advantage of two additional front buttons and two back ones, for a total of six action buttons. The SEGA Mega Drive (right) had a more ergonomic shape. There were only three action buttons, but they were higher performing.

TRICKS AND STRATEGY GUIDES

By 1987, kids all over the world weren't playing video games—they were playing "Nintendo." The NES and its games had consolidated their hold on the market, and young players were challenged to find strategies and techniques to progress through the latest titles, which could be quite complicated. Arcade games could only last a few minutes for economic reasons, but it was a whole different story at home. The adventures became more complex and the levels more numerous, and it took thinking and exploration to find your way through them. What to do if you couldn't find the solution? Today, there is YouTube. Back then, Nintendo recognized the problem and created an army of consultants with a single goal: to help gamers overcome every obstacle. It was an excellent strategy. Nintendo Game Play, the company's official support hotline, was buried in phone calls. The consultants needed to know every game and every level in detail; sometimes they used hand-drawn charts as guides. In 1988, Nintendo began publishing *Nintendo Power*, a specialized magazine for video gamers. Among its most important features were the level maps that gamers could use to orient themselves while playing. At that point, even the most difficult video games no longer held any secrets, and anyone could brag to his or her friends, "Haven't you finished *Zelda* yet?"

The cover of the first issue of *Nintendo Power* (July/August 1988), dedicated to the release of *Super Mario 2*. You can browse through many issues for free by scanning the QR code.

NINTENDO POWER ™

July/August 1988 $3.50

Super Mario 2
20-Page Spectacular

Zelda – Second Quest
In-Depth Review

Baseball Roundup

Over 50 Pro Tips

Free Poster Inside

Nintendo THE SOURCE FOR NES PLAYERS STRAIGHT FROM THE PROS

WOLFENSTEIN 3D
THE FIRST-PERSON SHOOTER ARRIVES

Immersion—the feeling that gamers expect and developers seek to provide—is almost taken for granted in today's video games. However, in the early nineties it was not so simple to create truly immersive video games; developers could only hope that the imagination would supply what technology could not yet provide. The turning point in the gaming experience came in 1992, when the id Software team, led by the visionary programmers John Romero and John Carmack, released *Wolfenstein 3D*. Thanks to its innovative graphics engine, the game popularized the first-person shooter (FPS) genre and the World War II subgenre. This laid the foundation for some of today's most popular franchises, including *Medal of Honor* and *Call of Duty*. *Wolfenstein 3D* still exemplifies the run-and-gun gameplay of modern FPS titles. The game introduced multiple important innovations: fluidly scrolling first-person visuals, a real revolution that literally changed the perception of video games; the protagonist's hand fixed at the center of the screen, aiming a gun at the enemy; and the ammunition count and personal arsenal that appear at the bottom of the screen.

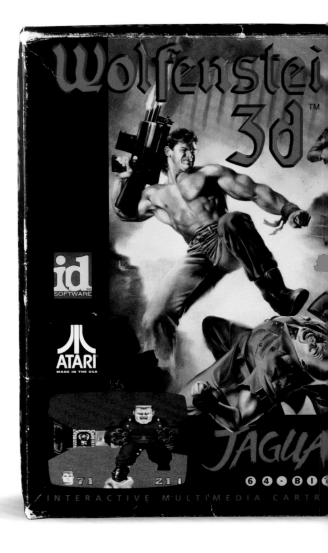

DOOM

THE APOCALYPSE IN A SHAREWARE VERSION

The success of *Wolfenstein 3D* also depended on another innovation: shareware distribution. Gamers could play for free until the end of the first episode, but they had to pay for the second and third ones. The next year, id Software released another first-person shooter, *Doom* (1993), using the same shareware model. For many, *Doom* was the FPS par excellence, with an improved graphics engine, a thrilling fluidity, and high-tension scenes of apocalyptic horror. Its new and spectacular weapons and claustrophobic spaces make *Doom* an enduring franchise even today.

LEFT: The Atari Jaguar version of *Wolfenstein 3D*. The graphics had much better resolution than the PC version and did not become blocky or pixelated when the player got close to the walls.

RIGHT: This Atari Jaguar version of *Doom* was the first official port of the original PC version, although the 32X version was released first. The 32X, 3DO, GBA, and PlayStation versions all derive from this one.

GRAPHIC ADVENTURES
POINT-AND-CLICK GAMING

Button combinations, coordination, speed, fast reflexes, and sometimes luck: these are what you need to win an arcade game. But do all video games need to have this fast-paced style of play? The answer arrived in the early nineties, when the first graphic adventures appeared on the market, descendants of the text-only adventure games from the early eighties. Graphic adventures, better known as "point-and-click" games, are narrative-based: the player must talk to various people, collect objects, and solve puzzles to move the story forward. It's like reading an adventure book, but with the ability, as the protagonist, to interact with the other characters and exercise your own skill and judgment. The graphic adventure genre was successful from the very first titles, like *Maniac Mansion* (1987) and *Zak McKraken* (1988) from LucasArts—which was, along with Sierra On-Line, the most important developer of point-and-click games. Over time, as the graphics and storylines were perfected, the genre reached high levels of engagement and immersion in series like Monkey Island (1990–2009), Space Quest (1986–1995), and Leisure Suit Larry (1987–2020), the last spiced up with a touch of eroticism. Unlike first-person shooters and fighting games, graphic adventures spread primarily among gamers who played on PCs and the Amiga 500.

Leisure Suit Larry III (1989). The first game in the series came out in 1987 and the latest in 2020, an extraordinarily successful run for a point-and-click franchise.

MONKEY ISLAND 2
A COMICAL TREASURE HUNT

Guybrush appears on the screen hanging from a rope and begins to recount his adventures to Elaine. So begins the second installment of *Monkey Island*. Everyone who played the first installment knew how many new puzzles awaited them in the sequel, which is still regarded as the high point of the series and one of the best graphic adventures of all time. This game, whose full title is *Monkey Island 2: LeChuck's Revenge* (1991), offers an irresistible mix of humor, surreal situations, references to other LucasArts titles, and above all, intricate puzzles to solve en route to the final treasure, called the "Big Whoop." It has a richer interface than the first *Monkey Island*, with a menu of nine possible actions (Give, Collect, Use, etc.) shown as text buttons, and a visual inventory of items possessed by the player. It also has two levels of difficulty: one with simpler puzzles, and the "complete" version. *Monkey Island 2* introduced more elastic gameplay, allowing the player to solve many puzzles nonsequentially. Even today, the first notes of the soundtrack recall those long summer afternoons when players needed only lower the blinds and insert a floppy disk into the drive to lose themselves on Scabb Island.

The first four installments of the Monkey Island series, created by Ron Gilbert in 1990. It became one of the longest-lasting point-and-click adventure franchises in the world.

AMIGA 500
THE HOME COMPUTER FOR GAMERS

Onstage in New York on July 23, 1985, with the aid of a digital camera and some innovative software, Andy Warhol created a portrait of Blondie singer Debbie Harry on a computer screen. The event was the launch of the Amiga 1000, the latest home computer from Commodore. Two years later, the company released a more compact version with various

improvements: the Amiga 500. The Advanced Multitasking Integrated Graphics Architecture, or Amiga for short, featured a cutting-edge architecture that offered greater computing power and multimedia capabilities than the Apple and IBM systems of the era, at a decidedly lower price. In short order, kids everywhere (but particularly in Europe) were asking their parents for

an Amiga 500. Video producers also flocked to the new system, due to its unique compatibility with television video formats and the innovative Video Toaster expansion card.

The gaming history of the Amiga is tied to graphic adventures like *Monkey Island*, but other titles took greater advantage of its multimedia power, from *Shadow of the Beast* (1989) to *Sensible Soccer* (1992, a real must-have before the advent of *FIFA* and *PES*). *Indianapolis 500* (1989), together with *Test Drive* (1991) and *Microprose Formula One Grand Prix* (1992), were the best driving simulators available, with a realism never seen before. The Amiga 500 contributed enormously to the gaming experience, moving beyond the model of the arcades. Now there began in earnest the development of new genres, including simulators, management and strategy games, puzzle games, and of course, graphic adventures. The emergence of all these new types of games had less to do with the advent of the 16-bit consoles than with advances in home computers.

The Amiga 500. Its code name, "B52/Rock Lobster," referring to the song "Rock Lobster" by the B-52s, was etched on the motherboard.

KEYBOARD AND MOUSE, OR GAMEPAD?

The gaming experience is certainly affected by the player's choice of peripherals. With the Commodore 64 and the ZX Spectrum, and even more with the Amiga 500, video gaming did not necessarily depend on lightning-fast reflexes. On these platforms, gaming assumed a new, more reflective form that rewarded logic, reason, and careful choices and thereby achieved a new kind of immersion. This development intensified one of the oldest debates in the world of gaming: which is better, the mouse and keyboard or the controller? Each has its fierce partisans, because this choice determines so much of the gaming experience. Undeniably, the keyboard brings a vast range of commands to hand, making it perfect for role-playing games or real-time strategy games. The mouse offers matchless precision in aiming at the enemy in an FPS game. On the other hand, the joystick or gamepad combines the characteristics of the keyboard and mouse into a single manageable object and is more comfortable for fighting or platform games. Essentially, the answer depends on the video game. Who knows how long this debate will go on?

STREET FIGHTER II
THE FIGHTING GAME WITH A CAPITAL F

The year 1991 was a fateful one for the video game industry. During those twelve months, Blizzard Entertainment (*Warcraft*, *Diablo*, *World of Warcraft*) and id Software (*Wolfenstein 3D*, *Doom*) were founded. SEGA introduced its mascot Sonic the Hedgehog and the Game Gear portable console. Games came out that were seminal for their genres, like *Lemmings* for the puzzlers and *Civilization* for turn-based strategy.

This year also saw the release of the definitive fighting game. Even today, *Street Fighter II* is considered the most important title in the genre; later innovations have been small and incremental. The first *Street Fighter* had allowed gamers to play only as a single character, the martial artist Ryu. But it had already introduced several new features to the genre, such as the ability to alternate between punches and kicks, to block the enemy's blows, and to use special moves like the Hadoken (an energy sphere) and the Shoryuken (a high uppercut). The second installment of *Street Fighter* raised the bar with other winning elements. The 16-bit architecture improved the graphics, fluidity, and music, while the robust storyline offered eight playable characters, each well developed. Gamers loved experimenting with the fighters' different capabilities and discovering the exact joystick and button sequences that yielded the special moves of Ryu, Ken, Blanka, Guile, E. Honda, Dhalsim, Zangief, and that unforgettable girl Chun Li. In single-player mode, the ultimate challenge was to beat the four final bosses, M. Bison, Vega, Sagat, and Balrog, who were controlled by the computer. Its appeal and longevity have made *Street Fighter II* Capcom's best-selling game, and today, after more than thirty years, it is still one of the most fascinating.

The Super Nintendo version of *Street Fighter II* (1992). The game's success endured into the new millennium with updated and enhanced versions.

NINTENDO PLAYSTATION
A MISSED OPPORTUNITY

Let's pause for a moment to think about how important the cartridge medium was to the history of gaming. Cartridges were the physical repositories of players' favorite games, and today they are sought-after collectibles. The transition from the cartridge to the CD-ROM was certainly not painless. Nintendo was reluctant to adopt the compact disc medium and committed themselves to developing their new Super Nintendo (1990) as a cartridge-based platform. However, they did not want to yield any technological advantage to SEGA, which had beaten them to the market with its own 16-bit cartridge-based console, the Mega Drive/Genesis (1988). So, as early as 1988, Nintendo entered into a secret collaboration with Sony to develop a new, CD-based version of its SNES. This yielded a prototype called the Nintendo PlayStation, which read both cartridges and CD-ROMs—an innovative console, probably without rival in its era. But Nintendo decided to withdraw from the collaboration in 1992, for reasons that were never made clear. As many as 200 units had already been distributed to developers, but after canceling the agreement, Nintendo raced to recall them for destruction. Only one machine was spared, and today it has become a cult object, exhibited at conventions, unique and precious. In 2020 its owner, Terry Diebold, put it up for auction, obtaining the incredible price of $360,000. Back in 1992, of course, Sony decided not to abandon the idea and continued development of a CD-based console on its own, giving rise, two years later, to the Sony PlayStation.

OPPOSITE: The prototype PlayStation entered development in 1988 but was canceled by Nintendo in 1992. This is the sole remaining example.

FOLLOWING PAGES: In the war between Super Nintendo (left) and SEGA Mega Drive (right)—known as the Genesis in North America—the exclusive games for each platform played an important role.

NEO GEO
BRINGING THE ARCADE HOME

In the 1990s, arcades were still a hangout for gamers and a place to discover the latest thing. At the beginning of that decade, the Japanese company SNK revolutionized the world of arcade cabinets with its Neo Geo MVS, a system that offered, in a single cabinet, one, two, four, or six games that could be switched out as easily as console cartridges. The arcade operators were happy, and so were the players. The inventory of games in this format was quite respectable, with titles like *Nam-1975* (1990), *Metal Slug* (1996), *Puzzle Bobble* (1994), and *Fatal Fury* (1991).

SNK's next winning move was to create a console based on the same hardware. The Neo Geo AES (1990) is still considered the Ferrari of consoles today, due to its remarkable fidelity to the arcade experience. The controller was an important factor, with its four buttons, joystick, and stability rivaling the control board of an arcade cabinet. The dream of bringing the arcade home had finally been realized! But at what price? The cost of the console alone was well over $500 in today's money—certainly not affordable for everyone.

OPPOSITE: The Neo Geo Advanced Entertainment System. Considered the Ferrari of consoles, it offered a gaming experience very similar to the arcades.

LEFT: The Neo Geo AES version of *Metal Slug* (1996).

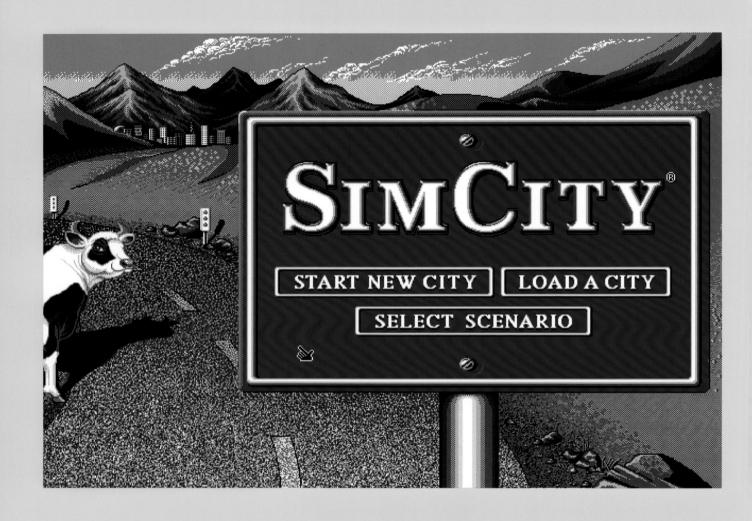

SIMCITY
BUILDING THE IDEAL METROPOLIS

Today, the gaming experience is more diverse than ever, encompassing a vast array of genres and subgenres. The nineties saw, among other innovations, the birth of the simulation genre, and in particular the managerial subgenre. The style of play in this type of video game is administrative. The player manages a complex structure or process, using strategy and planning skills rather than the quick reflexes required by arcade games. In *SimCity* (1989), the progenitor of the genre, the goal is to create and administer an entire city—in effect, to run a municipal government. Players must take steps to promote their citizens' welfare, from building housing and infrastructure to preventing natural disasters and collecting the taxes needed to fund municipal services. *SimCity* enjoyed great success, quickly becoming a model for other developers. Other successful titles along these lines included *Theme Park* (1994), *Theme Hospital* (1997), and even *The Sims* (2000), which simulated the lives of everyday people.

The unmistakable opening screen of the first *SimCity* (1989), a pioneer in the simulation genre and precursor of more recent titles like *The Sims* (2000).

FIFTH GENERATION

THE ADVENT OF THE CD-ROM AND THE LAN PARTY

Memory, always more memory! While Nintendo expanded to 64 bits, innovators focused on the "infinite" storage of the CD-ROM. In 1994, Commodore went under, and the PlayStation arrived. This was the era of *The Need for Speed*, the hundred-million-copy best seller, but also the artistic beauty of the tracks of *Gran Turismo*, the Venetian canals of *Tomb Raider 2*, the Arctic scenery of *Metal Gear Solid*, and the steampunk of *Final Fantasy 7*. Gamers discovered the ergonomics of the PlayStation controller and experimented with multiplayer gaming, hosting LAN parties for *Marathon* and *Quake*. With the fiasco of Virtual Boy, Nintendo learned that virtual reality must wait. Not so the Tips & Tricks, the secret weapons hidden in the code. The century ended with the question, "Is *The Legend of Zelda: Ocarina of Time* the best game ever?" Z-targeting and context-sensitive commands said yes.

FROM ROM TO CD-ROM

In the nineties, the gaming experience took another leap forward in quality. The fifth generation of consoles is mainly remembered for the rise of 3D graphics, but this would not have been possible without the advent of the CD-ROM. Obviously, 3D graphics already existed; they were common on PCs by the mid-nineties. However, the relatively smaller storage capacity of cartridges (also known as ROMs) could not support 3D video games worthy of the name. Here the apparently infinite capacity (for the era) of the CD came into play. CD-ROMs reached the gaming world in 1988, with the CD-ROM^2 add-on for NEC's PC Engine. The first personal computer game to be released on CD, in 1989, was the Mac-based graphic adventure *Manhole*, which had first come out on floppy disk a year earlier. A few years later, thanks to the potential of 3D graphics and the CD-ROM, the same developers brought out one of the most engaging video games of the nineties: *Myst* (1993). The goal of Ryan and Robin Miller, who led the development team, was to create a graphic adventure with more involving gameplay. Players could immerse themselves in a parallel world and interact with it in the most realistic manner possible. The use of a first-person perspective, which increased the player's identification with the game, was emblematic of this new kind of graphic adventure. The basic concept was this: to be catapulted into an unknown and, in certain ways, disquieting world, and to find your way home by solving a series of puzzles, without any tools at your disposal. Entertainment was assured.

Some leading CD-ROM games for the Panasonic 3DO. From the top, the first installment of *The Need For Speed*, the blockbuster driving series; the CD version of the classic *Dragon's Lair*, which first came out on Laserdisc in 1983; and, finally, *Myst*, the interactive graphic adventure that helped show the multimedia potential of the CD-ROM.

3DO

A DREAM SOON BROKEN

In 1993, while dinosaurs invaded the movie theaters, other colossi, like Nintendo and SEGA, were noticing the effect of the CD-ROM on the gaming world. The house of *Super Mario* remained skeptical about the medium, but its competitor SEGA marketed the Mega CD (1991), an add-on for the Mega Drive to read compact discs. NEC did the same thing for its PC Engine, even earlier. But the first console created specifically for the new medium was the 3DO (1993).

Trip Hawkins, founder of Electronic Arts, conceived of this new and futuristic 32-bit console. He pitched the idea to different manufacturers, including Panasonic, LG (Goldstar at the time), Sanyo, and Creative, and multiple companies produced 3DO systems under license. The system's CD-ROM drive and other advanced hardware allowed not only the development of 3D graphics but also the incorporation of high-quality soundtracks and full-motion video with cinematic production values. *The Need for Speed* (1994), *Star Control 2* (1992), and *Alone in The Dark* (1992) were among the titles released for the 3DO, which, however, did not have much success. Hawkins was right about the potential of the CD-ROM and multimedia, and the 3DO gaming experience was superior to that of any other system of the day, but the prohibitive price tag (about $700) did not help sales. The 3DO dream lasted only three years. In any case, kids the world over would soon find a viable alternative: the PlayStation.

Panasonic 3DO (1993), the first console to take full advantage of the CD-ROM medium. Its other innovations included a complex operating system, internal storage, and the ability to play video CDs.

THE NEED FOR SPEED
FLUID, IMMERSIVE GAMEPLAY

T he new three-dimensional graphics, enabled by the storage capacity of the CD-ROM and other technical advances, revolutionized driving simulators. It was exciting for motoring fans to drive powerful cars on roads that were dramatically more realistic than those in the racing games of the eighties. In *The Need for Speed* (1994), developed by Electronic Arts exclusively for the 3DO and later ported to the Sony PlayStation and SEGA Saturn, the graphics were arcade-quality and the tracks were incredibly accurate. The developers collaborated with automotive journalists to re-create as faithfully as possible the way the road held, the effects of acceleration and braking, and even the sounds of the driving environment. It goes without saying that the game was a success, and the Need for Speed series continues even today, with more than 100 million copies sold.

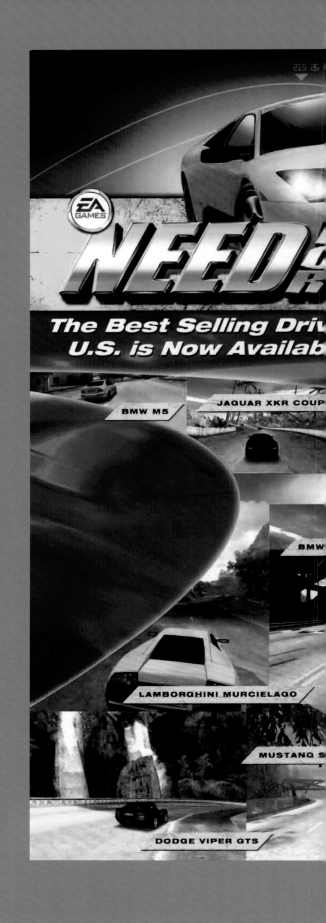

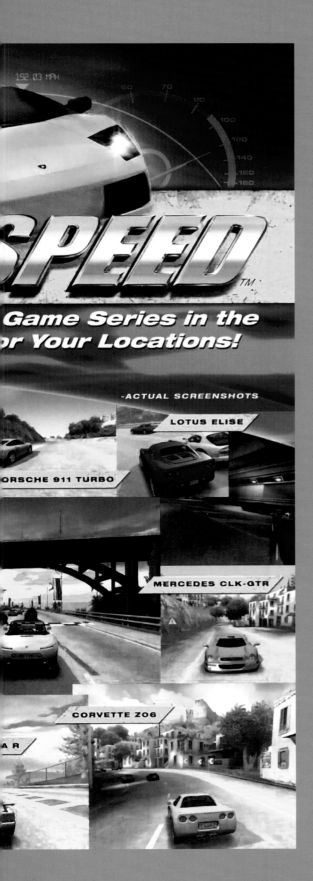

SPEED™

Game Series in the
[f]or Your Locations!

-ACTUAL SCREENSHOTS

LOTUS ELISE

[P]ORSCHE 911 TURBO

MERCEDES CLK-GTR

CORVETTE Z06

The Need for Speed was more than a living-room game—it carved out a space for itself in the arcades, too. This iconic game, with its variants and sequels, also inspired a Hollywood movie.

LIVE IN YOUR WORLD.
PLAY IN OURS.

In the years when teenagers were listening to Enimem, the gaming world underwent dramatic change. Even as the historic firm of Commodore was closing its doors in 1994, Sony shook the Japanese market with an earthquake: the PlayStation. For reasons both technical (the CD-ROM and the 32-bit processor) and commercial (intelligent marketing and aggressive advertising), Sony carved out a space in the video game market. The famous TV slogans "Live in your world. Play in ours" (in North America) and "Do not underestimate the power of PlayStation" (in Europe) sent expectations sky-high, even though the console would not arrive in those markets until September 1995. Who doesn't remember its famous start-up sound? A futuristic diamond followed by something that looks like a crystal sphere dashing itself on the ground, previewing the acoustic potential that only the PlayStation chip could offer.

With the power of its hardware and its exceptional catalog of titles, the first Sony-branded console raised the bar for the gaming experience. The world of PlayStation included the splendid tracks of *Gran Turismo* (1997), the Venetian canals of *Tomb Raider 2* (1997), the beautiful Arctic settings of *Metal Gear Solid* (1998), and the steampunk of *Final Fantasy 7* (1997). PlayStation showed that the video game could not be confined to a handful of anthropomorphic pixels.

Sony sold more than 102 million units of the original PlayStation in its several variations, which included the Net Yaroze, a black PlayStation that came with instructions and tools for developing video games at home. Pictured is the smaller PS One variant released in 2000.

THE PLAYSTATION CONTROLLER
A NEW GAMING TOOL

There had to be a reason the first PlayStation sold 102 million units by 2006. Maybe several reasons. One of the most important innovations had to with the gamepad. The PlayStation controller had a new shape, but once you took it in hand, you couldn't live without it. Its ergonomic grip was different from that of any other controller. Nintendo may have invented the directional cross and the diamond-shaped arrangement of buttons, but it was Sony that realized the shape of the gamepad needed to be as comfortable and solid as possible in the hands. Being able to hold the controller firmly while keeping the thumbs free proved to be the winning factor. The index and middle fingers also came into play: while most controllers had only one or two side buttons, the PlayStation had four (L1, L2, R1, and R2). From then on, this would be the standard for all gamepads. Later versions of this fantastic controller were equipped with two small joysticks in the center of the pad, which could be used in place of the directional cross. This solution allowed for more precise movement in many titles—and improved the gameplay of first-person shooters in particular.

The PlayStation 1 controller went through various iterations, including the DualShock pictured here, which vibrated in response to blows inflicted by the enemy.

GAMING THROUGH THE WIRE

nother turning point in gaming came when Local Area Networks (LANs) and then the Internet opened the way to online multiplayer games. Multiplayer gaming took off in 1994 with the release of *Marathon*, one of the first games developed by Bungie, which would score a blockbuster several years later with *Halo*. *Marathon* was a first-person shooter set aboard a space colony almost eight hundred years in the future. Despite its graphical limitations, this Macintosh-based game gained popularity for its multiplayer mode that supported LAN parties, a new type of networked gaming. Players would gather in a single location, hook their computers together with Ethernet cables, and

challenge each other in the games that supported this type of play. LAN games saw another, more dramatic increase in popularity in 1996, with the arrival of *Quake*, the blockbuster FPS from id Software. The release of the Windows 95 operating system and the spread of Ethernet cards also contributed to the rise of multiplayer LAN games, which brought the social aspect of gaming to a new level and laid the foundation for multiplayer games on a larger scale. But, even though CERN made the software for the World Wide Web available in the public domain on April 30, 1993, it would be several years before the Internet grew powerful enough to host the online games we know today.

LEFT: A screenshot from *Marathon* (1994), one of the first games to support LAN parties.

OPPOSITE: Nintendo 64, the console that tried to counter the rise of Sony's CD-based PlayStation by maximizing the potential of cartridges.

GOLDENEYE 007
A BENCHMARK FOR CONSOLE SHOOTERS

Although the gaming world hailed the CD-ROM as the new standard, Nintendo continued undeterred down its path strewn with cartridges, even into the 64-bit era. Who didn't love the Nintendo 64 (1996)? Many of the best games of that generation were exclusive to the N64. For example, *Super Mario 64* (1996), with its 3D open world, is considered one of the mustachioed plumber's best outings, if not one of the best video games ever. One unexpected title deserves mention: *GoldenEye 007* (1997)—the official video game of the James Bond movie of that name—in which one must fight a criminal organization that intends to destroy London and cause the collapse of the world economy. This first-person shooter offered not only single-player campaigns but the multiplayer death match, in which two or more players would face off against each other on the same console, with the screen divided into four displays. On a fifteen-inch TV, the action could be hard to follow, but it was still a powerful breakthrough. *GoldenEye 007* is regarded as a milestone in first-person shooters—proof that consoles could handle this genre, which had been considered suitable only for personal computers. Even today, players trying this title for the first time can't help but recognize its potential, despite the fact that it comes from the long-ago year of 1997.

THE FIRST ATTEMPTS AT VIRTUAL REALITY

The *Lawnmower Man* came out in theaters in 1992, drawing attention to a relatively little-known technology that would prove fascinating to video gamers in particular: virtual reality. In the movie, a scientist subjects a mentally challenged groundskeeper to a unique experiment, attempting to raise his IQ using drugs and virtual reality. The poor groundskeeper becomes a phenomenal video gamer and develops superpowers, like telepathy and telekinesis.

To try to jump on the virtual reality fad, Nintendo launched Virtual Boy (1995). Developed by Gunpei Yokoi, creator of the Game Boy, Virtual Boy was the first gaming system to offer, through its goggles, true three-dimensional graphics with the illusion of depth—but it was also Nintendo's most resounding commercial failure. In theory, the gaming experience should have been more immersive and engaging than on a normal screen. In reality, the graphics were displayed on a red monochrome screen, with a vague effect of depth that, perhaps because of a low refresh rate, produced a feeling of drunkenness and nausea after a few games. Some players developed headaches. The games did not take full advantage of the system's three-dimensional capabilities and failed to deliver a genuine virtual-reality gaming experience. Many more years would pass before VR would truly add a new dimension to gaming.

OPPOSITE: Virtual Boy, developed by Gunpei Yokoi, was one of Nintendo's most sensational flops.

RIGHT: *Mario Clash* was one of just twenty-three games developed for Virtual Boy.

TIPS + TRICKS
THE CHEATER'S CRAFT

The increasing difficulty of video games led programmers to build in hidden powers and options: for example, unlimited lives or resources, secret weapons, or even immortality. Special codes were needed to unlock these bonuses. Before the era of widespread Internet access, the only way to get these codes was to swap them with classmates or seek them out in the "Tips & Tricks" section of video game magazines. Some tricks required a special device that was inserted between the console and the cartridge. The most famous of these was Game Genie (1990), released first for the NES in 1990 and later for the Game Boy, SNES, Game Gear, and Mega Drive. Playing in cheat mode inevitably changed the gaming experience. On the one hand, having infinite lives made it possible to complete even the most difficult video games. On the other hand, it devalued the skills needed to progress through the levels and defeat the final boss. Often, the fun of the gameplay is its difficulty. Overcoming your limits as a gamer by practicing and developing your skills is part of the gaming experience. How many of us would admit to finishing *Ecco The Dolphin* (1993) with a list of codes?

Some versions of the Game Genie, a line of cartridges for various consoles that added cheat codes to games.

THE LEGEND OF ZELDA: OCARINA OF TIME

What is the best video game of all time? It's almost impossible to pick just one title, but many gamers, developers, and critics have called *The Legend of Zelda: Ocarina of Time* (1998) the best ever, not only for its artistic value but also for its influence on the world of gaming. Just as many fantasy novels and movies owe everything to Tolkien, this installment of *Zelda* introduced mechanisms and puzzles that proved seminal for later games—and it also marked a milestone in the transition to 3D graphics.

One of the most celebrated innovations of *Ocarina of Time* was Z-targeting. By pressing the Z button on the joypad of the Nintendo 64, the player could "hook" an enemy to center it onscreen and direct all attacks at it. Z-targeting is today so omnipresent that it is hard to imagine virtual fighting without it. But that was not the only innovation. When the number of commands exceeded the number of buttons on the gamepad, the normal solution was to use the "function" key. *Ocarina* presented a more elegant solution: a button that changed its function according to the circumstances. The A ("action") button was also the ALL button. It could make Link jump onto

his trusty mare Epona, launch a bomb, pull up grass to find rupees. . . . Context-sensitive commands extended also to actions that did not require a button, such as jumping over a fence. Solving puzzles to advance the story was not new, but the mechanisms or objects that

The principal titles in the Legend of Zelda series. The Japanese version of the original *Legend of Zelda* incorporated voice commands, taking advantage of the microphone in the Famicom pad.

the player could use were. Countless games have copied the idea of the Lens of Truth, which revealed hidden objects. It would take more than one book to list all the characteristics and curiosities of *Ocarina of Time*, which today is still a benchmark for gaming. And note that

its closest rival in the pantheon of all-time best video games is *Breath of the Wild* (2017), another Zelda installment, which amplified all the features of its predecessors and literally took the player into another dimension.

SIXTH GENERATION

POLYGONS, TEXTURES, AND MULTI-PLAYER ONLINE GAMES

1998-2005

With the turn of the new millennium, video games grew up. The gaming public had gotten older, and the titles evolved to suit it. On one hand there was the explorable world of *Shenmue*, which introduced the simulation of everyday life; on the other, the new first-person shooters, which included massive successes like *Halo* and *Call of Duty*. The two trends evolved to a point where they were no longer for children. *Final Fantasy X* was almost cerebral, offering a world to discover, while *Grand Theft Auto* portrayed the gratuitous violence of street crime. The sixth generation of consoles also marked a decisive move toward multiplayer online games, but not even the release of the Xbox and its Live service could beat the PlayStation 2. Extending a hand to the mainstream games of the recent past through backward compatibility, the PS2 sold more than three times as many units as the Microsoft Xbox, Nintendo GameCube and SEGA Dreamcast combined!

SEGA DREAMCAST
AN ARCADE IN YOUR OWN HOME

If hearing the name Dreamcast makes your heart skip a beat, you probably owned one. Almost surely, you think it was one of the best consoles ever sold. It came out in 1998, launching the sixth generation of consoles and approaching fidelity to the arcades. Remember *Sega Rally 2* (1999), *The House of The Dead 2* (1999), or *Soulcalibur* (1999)? The Dreamcast introduced many novelties, including an integrated modem that allowed players to challenge each other all over the world on titles like *Phantasy Star Online* (2000), an RPG designed specifically for online gaming. The Dreamcast also included a surprising data storage system: the Visual Memory Unit, a cartridge that was inserted directly into the gamepad and had its own black-and-white LCD display. You could play a minigame on the display, without the console. Friends could even swap saved games by connecting their VMUs. But these new features were not enough to ensure the success of the Dreamcast. Instead, slow sales led SEGA to exit the console market, although they continued to develop video games.

The Dreamcast, the last console produced by SEGA before the firm devoted itself exclusively to video game development. Accessories for the Dreamcast included a unit with a microphone that turned it into a karaoke machine.

SHENMUE
SIMULATING EVERYDAY LIFE

On December 29, 1999, while the world prepared to confront the feared millennium bug (an IT defect that would supposedly cause computers worldwide to malfunction when the year 2000 started), one of the most interesting adventure games for the SEGA Dreamcast was released in Japan. In addition to telling a moving and engaging story, *Shenmue* introduced new elements to the gameplay. Eighteen-year-old Ryo Hazuki is looking for his father's murderer, and must persevere through fights, chases, motorcycle races, and various minigames in a completely explorable world. The developer's name for this kind of open-world gaming, which simulated many aspects of everyday life, was Full Reactive Eyes Entertainment (FREE). The realism of the passage of time is impressive, and the presence of characters going about their own business in their virtual lives is intriguing. Everything is built to seem real: even the weather reproduces the climatic conditions of the region of Japan where the game is set!

WHERE HAVE I SEEN RYO BEFORE?

Maybe you're asking yourself where you've already seen Ryo, the protagonist of *Shenmue*. The creator of the game, Yu Suzuki, has always said that *Shenmue* was intended to be an RPG with the characters from *Virtua Fighter*, so we know for sure that the resemblance between Ryo and Akira from the SEGA fighting game is not a coincidence.

Shenmue was one of SEGA's most ambitious video games. Its development cost about $47 million.

BELOW: PlayStation 2. During its commercial lifetime, about 4,500 video games were released for it, making it the console with the largest game library of all time, as well as the best seller.

RIGHT: The opening screen of *Metal Gear Solid 2: Sons of Liberty*. Hideo Kojima has always said that his protagonist Solid Snake was inspired by Snake Plissken, hero of the movie *Escape from New York*.

PLAYSTATION 2
THE ALL-TIME BEST SELLER

If there is one console that changed the world of gaming, it is certainly the PlayStation 2. Thanks to its cultural, technological, and social impact, Sony's second console became the biggest seller of all time, with more than 157 million units shipped. Sony's decision to make the PS2 backward compatible was a stroke of genius. PlayStation 1 owners who had amassed a sizable collection of games had an incentive to remain loyal to Sony—and a guarantee that they could still use their old DualShock controllers. For those who did not already own a PlayStation, the PS2 was the perfect buy-in point, as a sixth-generation machine that could read fifth-generation games. PlayStation 2 buyers could take advantage of the greatest variety of console games ever, with mainstream successes like *Metal Gear Solid 2: Sons of Liberty* (2001), *Gran Turismo 4* (2004), and *Grand Theft Auto: San Andreas* (2004); artistic and original adventures like *Ico* (2001) and *Shadow of the Colossus* (2005); and curiosities like *Katamari Damacy* (2004). This is why the PS2 sold three times as many units as the Microsoft Xbox, Nintendo GameCube, and SEGA Dreamcast combined.

GRAND THEFT AUTO: SAN ANDREAS
RISE OF THE SANDBOX GAME

Few franchises have established a new frame of reference for the gaming world like Grand Theft Auto. Despite being labeled morally harmful, GTA revolutionized almost everything, from gameplay to the use of music, narration, violence, and setting. Looking back, it is apparent that the influence of GTA has extended to every corner of popular culture: movies, TV, music videos, and even fashion.

The fifth installment of the series, *Grand Theft Auto: San Andreas* (2004), released initially for the PlayStation 2, was the best-selling video game for sixth-generation consoles. In *San Andreas*, the player assumes the role of an outlaw who must carry out criminal missions in the city of Los Santos: kidnappings, murders, fencing stolen goods, and many others. The 3D installments of the series—*GTA III* (2001) and onward—are considered among the first "sandbox games": games that offer the player many tools and possibilities, and allow them to explore and even alter the game environment without limiting them to a particular mission or objective. In the open world of GTA, everything is possible, and nothing is predictable. The thrill of the forbidden has made it an explosive franchise even today, with the release of each installment attracting millions of players.

A child playing *Grand Theft Auto*. Published by Rockstar Games, the franchise has been revolutionary in multiple respects, but its content has also made it controversial.

NO-HOLDS-BARRED VIOLENCE

Video games have long been criticized for their violent content, even before the arrival of Grand Theft Auto. Gamers relished titles like *Doom*, *Mortal Kombat*, and *Duke Nukem* specifically for their outrageous content and graphics. However, the violence in Grand Theft Auto was different from that of other video games. First, it was more realistic and less cartoonish. In GTA, you don't shoot a plasma blaster at aliens, and you don't fight robots in a fantasy martial arts tournament. Instead, you run over a pimp with your car, or you kill a rival pusher, as really happens in criminal life. Second, the violence in Grand Theft Auto is considered more egregious: beating up someone with a baseball bat instead of paying them is more outrageous to most people than throwing a grenade from the trenches at an enemy on the battlefield. The "total" violence of Grand Theft Auto is different from anything seen before or since, because it is closer to the real thing. For critics of video games, GTA exemplifies their pernicious influence on adolescents. For many players, it confirms that video games are headed in the right direction.

TOP: Scorpion executes his famous "get over here" move on Raiden in the original arcade version of *Mortal Kombat* (1992).

BOTTOM: A gunfight with the police in *Grand Theft Auto: San Andreas* (2004).

THE IMPACT OF XBOX LIVE

The year 2001 is remembered in history for the tragic attacks of September 11 and the beginning of the global War on Terror, but on a less serious note, it also marked the entrance of Microsoft into the world of gaming. The Xbox was the first console with an internal hard disk drive, and it was also the most powerful gaming device on the market, thanks to its Pentium III

processor. But the Xbox made the greatest impact with its online gaming service. Xbox Live was introduced in 2002 and completely changed the gaming industry and the way games were played. It allowed players to challenge each other from home over a broadband connection. The acronym MMO (Massively Multiplayer Online) was coined to describe those games that allowed thousands of players to connect simultaneously to a persistent virtual world. Before the Xbox Live, MMO games were mostly confined to PCs and not available on consoles.

To date, Microsoft has built the Xbox Live subscriber base to about 120 million users. The online game has become a focus of culture and innovation, and, naturally, an enormous business opportunity: it took Sony until 2006 to release its own version of Xbox Live, the PlayStation Network, but it now has just as many subscribers. Online games can also be more profitable for developers, not only because they have the potential to sell more copies, but also because they generate additional revenue through in-game sales of additional features and content.

Microsoft Xbox, the first console from the colossus of Redmond. It was so large that gamers jokingly called it a "VCR."

FINAL FANTASY X

Every fan of role-playing games knows the Final Fantasy franchise, one of the most popular of all time. But as with most great video game franchises, there is one installment that stands out above the rest. *Final Fantasy X* (2001) immerses its players in a new world, more mature in terms of both design and gameplay, with three-dimensional environments to explore instead of simple pre-drawn backgrounds. It is also the first game in the series to feature complete voice-overs. In many ways, it set the course for the video games of the last two decades.

OPPOSITE: Two cosplayers at MCM London Comic Con 2016 portraying Tidus and Yuna, the protagonists of *Final Fantasy X.*

BELOW: A screenshot from the game, showing the cosplayers' inspiration.

THE AUDIENCE CHANGES

In the new millennium, teenagers and young adults began to outnumber younger children in the gaming population. The industry had already been shifting toward more "adult" games since the 16-bit era, but in the sixth generation it made this leap in earnest. Dark and violent titles like *God of War* (2005), *Resident Evil 4* (2005), and the Grand Theft Auto series redefined the boundaries of interest in video games. For example, Nintendo suffered from its reputation as a maker of casual games aimed at children. The toylike appearance of the GameCube (2000) contributed to this impression. On the other hand, Sony and Microsoft had a more "hardcore" image, thanks to the many violent action games released for their consoles. It should be noted, though, that the sixth generation was not characterized by any single genre of games. Yes, players could test themselves in battles to the death in first-person shooters like *Counter-Strike* (1999), *Halo* (2001), and *Call of Duty* (2003). But there were also many third-person shooters, not to mention platformers, RPGs, and sports games. A number of games that did not fit into any single genre enjoyed success as well. One could even say that the sixth generation offered the richest variety of games.

Kratos, the protagonist of *God of War* (2005). His name was chosen shortly before the game's release, replacing the original "Dominus."

GAMECUBE
A FAREWELL TO THE CARTRIDGE

In 2000, expectations for the Nintendo GameCube were high. The Nintendo 64 had not sold as well as previous Nintendo consoles, but with *Mario 64*, *Ocarina of Time*, and *GoldenEye 007*, Nintendo had some of the best fifth-generation games. Now the cartridge was replaced with a proprietary mini-DVD format, which discouraged piracy but also prevented users from watching DVDs or listening to music CDs (as they could on other platforms, like the PlayStation 2). The GameCube was much less expensive than its rivals, but at the time of its release, the best-loved and most iconic Nintendo franchises were not yet available on it. It was up to LucasArts' *Star Wars: Rogue Leader* (2000) to show off the graphic capabilities of the machine, and, ironically, to SEGA's *Super Monkey Ball* to convey the Nintendo "feel."

The Nintendo GameCube (2000) with a wired controller. There was also a wireless version, the first offered by a console manufacturer, that used two AA batteries and lacked the vibration feedback mechanism.

1998–2005

SEVENTH GENERATION

THE VIDEO GAME AS ART

2004-2012

ell before the Museum of Modern Art took notice, video games were becoming the Eighth Art, combining the cinematic and the interactive. Increased computing power enabled the creation of intricate virtual worlds, a feature shared by such disparate games as *Assassin's Creed Origins, God of War*, and *Call of Duty: WWII*. *Minecraft* dragged video games from the realm of pure entertainment. Players could meet and interact in worlds they built themselves, and this constructive, social type of interaction carried over into many online titles that came out later. But that wasn't all: in the educational edition of *Minecraft*, children could learn to code, combine atoms into molecules, and re-create historic buildings. The rise of indie distribution platforms and motion control, which countered the stereotype of the sedentary gamer, also signaled profound changes in gaming.

TOWARD RECOGNITION AS THE EIGHTH ART

In the third millennium, it is no longer heresy to consider video games an art form. In seventh-generation games, animation, storytelling, characterization, and voice acting acquired a realism previously only seen in the movies. However, as an art form, the video game also has a unique feature: interactivity. Consecration arrived in 2012, when the Museum of Modern Art in New York acquired fourteen video games—from *Pong* (1972) and *Asteroids* (1979) to *Portal* (2007) and *Minecraft* (2011)—and displayed them in a design exhibition. By the end of the seventh generation, games like *The Last of Us* (2013) became true cultural phenomena, thanks to the emotional realism of their characters and the solid writing of their storylines. Even Hollywood actors lent their faces to video games. This was possible because of the power of the consoles: the PlayStation 3 and Xbox 360 could process hundreds of thousands of polygons simultaneously, and the graphics approached a photographic level of realism. Players could now identify with the protagonists of the game, who appeared much more human than in the past.

The *Pac-Man* installation at the Museum of Modern Art in New York. *Pac-Man* was among the video games that the museum acquired for its permanent collection of architecture and design, as examples of excellence in interactive design.

MINECRAFT
CREATE YOUR WORLD AND YOUR ADVENTURE

Imagine overturning a bucket of virtual Lego blocks and building anything you want with them. This was the concept of *Minecraft* (2009), a world of blocks to create adventures with. Fifteen years and 300 million copies later, *Minecraft* is the best-selling video game of all time. There are various ways to play the game: for example, in survival mode, players must gather natural resources, like wood and stone, to build key items.

    Minecraft was designed for everyone, and it has influenced gaming forever. *Assassin's Creed Origins*, *God of War*, and *Call of Duty: WWII*: what do all these games have in common? A "crafting" system, just like *Minecraft*'s. Its gameplay, centered on creation and construction in order to survive, has inspired other games with the same internal dynamics. So where the developers once created all the worlds, stories, and adventures, now the players can do it themselves in *Mario Maker* or *Fortnite* as well as in *Minecraft*. *Minecraft* has also shaped the social development of gaming. Players can meet and interact in their self-constructed worlds, and this social aspect has been adopted in many subsequent online games.

2004–2012

The perception of the social role of video games is changing. In Stary Oskol, Russia, a boy plays *Minecraft* while getting a haircut.

THE EDUCATIONAL VALUE OF GAMING

arents and children's advocacy groups have often underscored the dangers of video games. But in recent years, perspectives have been changing. Learning the periodic table might normally be boring, but with *Minecraft* it's a different story. *Minecraft Education* was released in 2016 and is now used by thousands of teachers worldwide. *Minecraft* can teach children how to code, identify plants and animals, and combine atoms into molecules to make new materials. Countless educational projects have arisen in the world of virtual blocks. In the Netherlands, for example, "RoMeincraft" allows young history students to re-create Roman buildings based on archaeological studies.

A CONSOLE WITH THE HEART OF A PC

At the beginning of the twenty-first century, experts agreed that the best platform for video gaming was the PC. With high-performance processors, unlimited RAM, and dedicated graphics cards, hardcore gamers could be the masters of the world. How did the console world react to all this power? Microsoft and Sony, the two principal competitors in the market, released new machines that, in terms of their technical features, were more or less PCs disguised as consoles. Although their hardware could not be updated as a PC's could, the Xbox 360 and the PlayStation 3 (both 2005) offered sufficient power to ensure very realistic graphics and hours of entertainment. So, was the war between PC enthusiasts and console lovers over? Absolutely not!

The Sony PlayStation 3 in its Fat and Slim versions. The first Fat versions were backward compatible with the PlayStation 2. The Slim was not, but it did have a new and more reliable Blu-ray reader.

2004-2012

THE RED RING OF DEATH
VS. THE YELLOW LIGHT OF DEATH

This is not a video game with a Tolkienesque setting. The Red Ring of Death refers to three or four red lights that flash in a ring around the power button when an Xbox 360 malfunctions. Depending on the number of lights flashing, the user may be able to recognize the problem and try to fix it before taking the machine to technical support. In most cases, four flashing lights indicate that the system has overheated.

The Microsoft Xbox 360. The development of the controller for the second Microsoft-branded console took ten years and cost $100 million. The keys of the gamepad can withstand more than three million presses.

Faithful fans of the PlayStation 3 face a similar system failure, called the Yellow Light of Death. This flashing yellow light on the front of the console usually appears when the thin layer of thermal paste between the motherboard and processor deteriorates, causing the the system to overheat and crash. Planned obsolescence? More likely, design errors and scrimping on raw materials.

PORTAL
A FIRST-PERSON PUZZLE GAME

In 2007, while Apple was launching the iPhone and ushering in the age of the smartphone, the video game industry was also trying to impress the world with new ideas. Crossover between video game genres was nothing new, but first-person shooters had seemed exempt from it. Then Valve Software—the firm that had developed *Half-Life* and *Counter-Strike* (both 1998)—released *Portal* (2007), a puzzle game presented in the graphical style of a first-person shooter. *Portal* takes place in a science-fiction setting full of dark humor; the protagonist, a young woman named Chell, is armed with a Portal Gun that can create portals between different physical locations. If the two ends of the portal are not located on the same plane, bizarre situations of physics and gravity can result.

Portal (2007), developed by Valve, met with critical acclaim for its original approach and innovative ideas.

A screenshot from *The Elder Scrolls IV: Oblivion* (2006).

At the Golden Joystick Awards 2006, the Take 2 Interactive team shows off the trophy for best game of the year, for *The Elder Scrolls IV: Oblivion*.

OPEN WORLDS

Unbounded worlds in which players could lose themselves adventuring—or just interacting with the environment—were popular in sixth-generation games. However, all this space for exploration forced a compromise in graphics and a sacrifice of detail. All this changed in the seventh generation. *GTA: San Andreas* (2004) raised the bar, but with *The Elder Scrolls IV: Oblivion* (2006) came the true leap in quality. This title offered an incredible number of skills and so many missions that it seemed like a master class in RPG mechanics. Completing all elements of the game required about 180 hours, of which just 20 to 30 were for the main plot. After *Oblivion*, expectations for open world play changed radically. Titles like *Oblivion* changed the nature of gameplay itself: players felt less urgency to reach higher levels and complete missions, and a greater desire to explore worlds that now seemed alive in all their aspects. This is why gamers today expect developers to fill their virtual worlds with beauty as well as challenges.

NINTENDO DS
A NEW LEVEL OF PORTABLE GAMING

The Game Boy grew up along with portable gaming, and it lasted in various forms until 2004, when it was set aside for a new and innovative platform. The Nintendo DS took mobile gaming to a new level, approaching console quality. It had a touchscreen years before the Apple iPhone, and its double-screen format allowed for more sophisticated graphics: for example, the player might see a first-person view on one screen and a top-down view on the other. Wireless connectivity enabled multiplayer gaming, with each player on his or her own device. Given that Nintendo sold 154 million units of the DS, they certainly did not regret retiring the Game Boy.

The Nintendo DS took its inspiration from the Game & Watch Multi Screen but looked to the future. One of the names considered for this console was City Boy.

THE INDIE SCENE TAKES OFF

As the Internet made its way into every home, and PCs and consoles were connected to the global network, digital distribution platforms like Xbox Live, PlayStation Network, and Steam grew in popularity. Developers with innovative ideas but few resources no longer faced the problem of manufacturing and distributing games on physical media. So, when the mainstream market began to reach its creative limits, small independent developers were able to come to the rescue. Two success stories spring to mind: *Bastion* (2011) and *Limbo* (2010), games that were released almost at the end of the seventh generation. The former is an action RPG; the latter, a puzzle-platformer. Both have a delightfully minimalist and original style. For video gamers, titles like these were a breath of fresh air. (Did you know that *Minecraft* also started as an independent video game?) The success of indie games gave the big developers the jolt they needed to recommit themselves to finding new ideas and creating ever more engaging gameplay.

2004—2012

LIMBO
ATMOSPHERIC GAMEPLAY

In a market where the expectations of users and the ambitions of developers focused on ever-larger open worlds and ever-more-realistic graphics, *Limbo* (2010) broke the rules. This title laid the groundwork for independent developers who were ready to create new gaming experiences from scratch. *Limbo* creates a disquieting atmosphere through graphics rendered in an almost suffocating black and white, with very little narrative or characterization. As a puzzle-platformer, inspired by titles like *World of Goo* (2008) and *Machinarium* (2009), it offers an absorbing series of physics-based challenges that must be overcome by trial and error, often with gory consequences. Even today, *Limbo* stands out for its ambience, its ingenious gameplay, and its cultural impact on developers.

Bastion (2011) is one of the best-loved indie titles. It owes its success to its dynamic storytelling and the originality of its hand-colored graphics.

2004–2012

MOTION CONTROL
A NEW GAMING EXPERIENCE

The essence of video gaming is to interact with what's happening on the screen. If you can do that by moving around in real space, the experience will be more engaging (and perhaps counter the stereotype of the sedentary gamer). That was the thinking of the developers who replaced the classic gamepad with a motion controller. The first to try was Nintendo, with the Wii (2006) and its Wii Remote, which looked like a TV remote and used an integrated accelerometer and an infrared sensor bar placed near the TV set to reproduce the player's movements onscreen.

But did motion control really improve the gaming experience? The success of *Wii Sports* (2006), the game bundled with the Wii and one of the best-selling titles of all time, certainly proved that it was an appealing novelty, and Nintendo's main competitors felt they had to experiment with motion control, too. In 2010, Sony released the PlayStation Move, a controller similar to the Wii Remote, equipped with a three-axis accelerometer, a three-axis angular rate sensor, a magnetometer to detect the Earth's magnetic field, and a vibration feedback mechanism. The Move could also use the PlayStation Eye, a webcam-like peripheral, to detect the player's position. Microsoft tried a different strategy with its Kinect (2010), which allowed the player to control the video game without wearing or holding anything: the optical and infrared cameras in the Kinect simply detected the player's movements and translated them to the screen. Motion control spawned at least one hit franchise—the Just Dance series—but user response was tepid overall, and most developers put the technology aside, awaiting better times. Maybe the advent of virtual reality. . . .

The Nintendo Wii. One of Barack Obama's 2008 presidential campaign ads urged viewers to put down their Wii Remotes and vote.

SUPER MARIO GALAXY

OUTER-SPACE ADVENTURE

It was very difficult for Nintendo and its Wii to compete with other seventh-generation consoles, like the Xbox 360 and PlayStation 3. Even though motion control was new and original, the Wii did not offer the same level of gameplay as its competitors. Then along came Mario, as usual, to raise the stakes. *Super Mario Galaxy*, the third 3D game in the Super Mario series, was released in 2007. It took full advantage of the Wii's unique hardware, establishing itself as one of the best games ever to feature the mustachioed plumber.

Charles Martinet, the longtime English-language voice of Mario and Luigi, poses with Mario at the UK launch of *Super Mario Galaxy*.

EIGHTH GENERATION

MOTION CAPTURE AND VIRTUAL REALITY

2 BILLION

F our factors drove gaming as the 2020s approached: the mobile explosion, motion capture, the MOBA (Multiplayer Online Battle Arena) phenomenon, and the relaunch of virtual reality. Mobile gaming, enabled by the spread of the smartphone, changed the way millions of people played video games, launching titles like *Angry Birds*—downloaded two billion times in 2014 alone. Motion capture has made digital animation much more fluid and realistic, not just in animated movies but in video games as well. The MOBA has given rise to global e-sports phenomena like the *League of Legends* World Championship. Finally, the relaunch of virtual reality might be able to offer the level of immersion that gamers have always sought—although for now it seems that the Oculus Rift and PlayStation VR are only a first step toward the goal of total engagement.

GAMING GOES MOBILE

Since the arrival of the smartphone and the app store in 2007, video games have once again evolved dramatically, not only in the way they are played but also in their impact on mainstream culture. Rapid developments in mobile technology in the second decade of the new millennium led to an explosion of games developed for the smartphone, with a sales volume exceeding that of console games. This enormous rise in mobile gaming, especially in Southeast Asia, not only expanded the demographics of gamers but caught the attention of the media. Whereas gamers once met up on newsgroups and forums, today they talk on social media. Apple and Google quietly moved up the ranks of video game retailers through their app stores. Titles in the Angry Birds series, launched in 2009, earned $200 million for Rovio (the Finnish company that developed it) in 2012 alone and exceeded two billion downloads in 2014. More complex online multiplayer games like *Clash of Clans* (2012) reported enormous earnings, connecting millions of players around the world through mobile devices.

ABOVE: *Angry Birds* (2009) is one of the most successful games originally developed for smartphones. Two billion downloads in 2014!

RIGHT: *Clash of Clans* (2012) is another example of video games creating culture: in 2016 it inspired an animated web series, *Clash-A-Rama*, which won the People's Voice Award at the 2019 Webbies.

POWER VS. INNOVATION

The transition to mobile technology has defined a new chapter in the history of video games. However, while smartphone games are well adapted to the frenetic life of millennials, they do have their limits. Phone screens are small, and the processor speeds and internal memories of most devices preclude highly complex games with advanced graphics. So, even though smartphones may have cut into the market for portable gaming devices, console sales continued to grow, and each new generation brought advances in technology and power.

The eighth generation of consoles opened with an ill-fated Nintendo console. With the Wii U (2012), Nintendo set out to create a console with its own screen, so kids could keep playing even when other family members were watching TV. The Wii U's controller had a large touchscreen, which served as a secondary screen when gamers could

use their TVs, and as the primary screen when they could not—although the controller had to remain within about twenty feet of the main console. The idea was not a big commercial success, even if it did enhance the gameplay of certain well-designed games. For example, *Batman: Arkham City—Armored Edition* (2012) and *Darksiders II* (2012)

The Nintendo Wii U. The best-selling game for this relatively unsuccessful console was *Mario Kart 8*, with 8.46 million copies sold, followed by *Super Mario 3D World* with 5.89 million and *New Super Mario Brothers U* with 5.82 million.

used the gamepad display for inventory or as a map while the action continued on the TV screen. However, the Wii U did lay the foundation for the development of the Nintendo Switch (2017), the first true hybrid console in history, which can be connected to the TV but also used outside the home. The Switch's two Joy-Con controllers can be attached to either side of its integrated screen, or detached from it and used either separately or in tandem. They also have motion control capabilities. Meanwhile, during these years, Microsoft and Sony challenged each other with the power of their Xbox One and PlayStation 4, releasing versions that supported 4K and HDR (High Dynamic Range) TV screens.

The Nintendo Switch, displaying art for *The Legend of Zelda: Breath of the Wild*. The console is designed for one or two players. In two-player mode, the blue and red Joy-Con controllers can be used separately.

THE LEGEND OF ZELDA
BREATH OF THE WILD

The world of Link and Princess Zelda has always been one of the best-loved and most-anticipated video game franchises. Although there are many excellent titles in the series, *Breath of the Wild* (2017) is the most complete realization of the "go anywhere" promise of open-world gaming. Many eighth-generation open-world console games continued along the same lines as *Assassin's Creed*, using their maps more as giant backdrops for the gameplay than as worlds worth exploring. *Breath of the Wild* inverted this trend. Its climbing system is limitless, and the completely unmarked map forces players to discover the reference points and interesting activities in the Kingdom of Hyrule for themselves. The result is a world in which a quiet trek along a rocky coast or the splendid view from a mountaintop is just as satisfying as fighting an enemy or solving a complicated puzzle.

2011–2021

MOTION CAPTURE
THE ILLUSION OF LIFE

By now, it has been years since our onscreen characters seemed to move only their legs, with the rest of their bodies remaining nearly static. In today's video games, motion capture technology is commonly used to reproduce the movements of human beings as faithfully as possible. The process involves recording the movements of an actual person and then mapping them onto a virtual character. Starting with the arcade game *Virtua*

Fighter 2 in 1994, developers have swiftly ramped up their use of motion capture, employing directors and appropriately cast actors—just as in a movie production. The underlying technology has also improved continuously, enabling simpler and smoother workflows for both indie developers and the biggest software companies. Its realistic rendering of movement is yet another factor in making games more immersive.

Quarterback Tom Brady participates in a motion capture session. The reflective markers positioned on his equipment helped animate his avatar in *ESPN NFL Football* (2003).

€10

ⓇBLOX

milioni di giochi
su Roblox

10€

LEAGUEof
LEGENDS

Riscattabile in League of Legends,
Teamfight Tactics,
Legends of Runeterra e VALORANT

LEAGU
LEGEN

Riscattabile in League o
Teamfight Tacti
Legends of Runeterra e

€20

ⓇBLOX

ca milioni di giochi
su Roblox

19,99€

FORTNITE®

2800 V-BUCK

INCLUDE IL
12%
EXTRA!

DISPOSITIVI SUPPORTATI¹

PLAYSTATION®, XBOX, NINTENDO SWITCH™,
PC, CELLULARI

12
www.pegi.info

FORTN

5000 V-BU

DISPOSITIVI SUPPORTATI¹

PLAYSTATION®, XBOX, NINTENDO SWITC
PC, CELLULARI

THE IMPACT OF MICROTRANSACTIONS

As video game budgets grew to rival those of Hollywood movies, developers needed to find new ways to recoup their costs. The single amount paid to buy the game was not enough. Downloadable content (DLC) emerged as a way to convince players to pay for add-ons to a game they had already purchased. It helped form a new type of video game market, foreshadowing the kind of microtransactions gamers are familiar with today.

A microtransaction is a business model in which users can purchase virtual objects within games for real money. They often occur in free-to-play games, which are free to download but require in-game purchases to advance or to develop one's character. Microtransactions have had a significant impact on gaming, but not without controversy: it is no accident that only an estimated 15 percent of gamers participate in microtransactions. One problem is that in-game purchases affect the gaming experience. Almost all the titles that offer microtransactions are online multiplayer games, and players who buy weapons, armor, or magic potions can count on having a stronger character than opponents who do not make these purchases. Inevitably, this makes the contest seem unfair, as its outcome depends not on the skill the player has acquired through hours of practice, but on the money the player has spent to build a stronger character without effort. While they are much criticized and compared to gambling for their ability to promote addictive spending, microtransactions probably won't disappear any time soon—although reducing them would help preserve a fair gaming experience.

Credits to obtain extra content within video games can be purchased in stores as well as online.

RED DEAD REDEMPTION 2
A NEW STANDARD FOR ADVENTURE

Have you ever thought about a video game when you weren't playing it? Or wanted to keep playing after you finished it? In the history of video games, few titles have inspired this kind of reaction. Scenic, far-reaching, and overpowering, with a level of detail that only multiple years of high-budget development can achieve, *Red Dead Redemption 2* (2018) transports players into a world that seems to have its own independent existence. While the sun rises and sets, the characters go about their routines, the buildings and railroad tracks grow, and the wildlife wanders through untamed lands. In these acres of picturesque landscape, players can lose themselves in hunting game or searching for treasure, or just exploring like tourists, forgetting about the main storyline for a few hours. But that storyline, concerning the protagonist Arthur Morgan's adventures with the Dutch Van Der Linde Gang, is equally fascinating. In creating a follow-up to one of the best games of the previous generation, Rockstar managed to outdo itself, reinventing the Western and setting a new standard for truly convincing immersion.

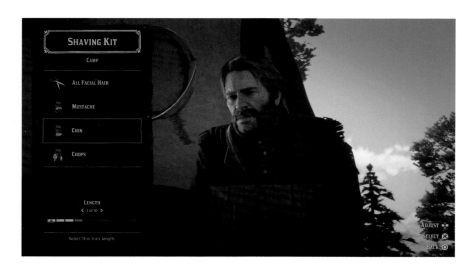

Red Dead Redemption 2. Arthur Morgan's beard grows in real time, and the player must take care of his physical appearance. Morgan must shave, get his hair cut, and even take a bath if he doesn't want to be shunned by the townspeople.

MMO VS. MOBA

[H]ow many of you and your friends regularly play online games? It's an ever more common pastime, and undoubtedly fun. Challenging opponents worldwide in real time is a way to share your passion, test your abilities against real people, and feel like part of a community. This experience, as we have seen, is defined by the acronym MMO, for Massively Multiplayer Online gaming. The biggest MMOs, like *World of Warcraft* (2004), *EVE Online* (2003), and *City of Heroes* (2005), have shaped the conventions of this rapidly growing

genre. But the MMOs have evolved and split into subgenres, like the MMORPG (online role-playing game) and, more recently, the MOBA (Multiplayer Online Battle Arena). If men are from Mars and women are from Venus, as John Gray writes in his famous book, then the

MMO and the MOBA must come from different galaxies. Notwithstanding the similarities between MMO maps and MOBA arenas, the two genres have adopted very different approaches to progression, persistence, and match-making. This split has led to two different but equally engaging ways for gamers to test themselves against human adversaries. In a MOBA, there is a closed map, and two opposing teams fight to destroy the enemy's base while preserving their own. *League of Legends* (2009) is one of the most successful examples, though it owes much to earlier titles like *StarCraft* (1998) and *Warcraft III: Reign of Chaos* (2002). Today, MOBAs are gaining ever more converts—not only players but also viewers of streaming channels and official competitions.

The finals of the 2015 *League of Legends* World Championship in Brussels. Team Fnatic faces the KOO Tigers.

2011—2021

FORTNITE
AN UNEXPECTED GLOBAL PHENOMENON

Love it or hate it, you can't deny that *Fortnite* (2017) is one of the most popular online games of all time. The very simple gameplay is based on a third-person shooter engine and offers various modes, including Save the World, Creative Mode, and Battle Royale. With more than 350 million registered users, this free-to-play game has become a mainstay of the gaming industry. Live *Fortnite* events boast millions of spectators, the top streamers attract their own sponsors, and the top players have made fortunes at tournaments. By now, *Fortnite* has become more than a game; it is a cultural phenomenon. Among other events, *Fortnite* has hosted concerts with artists at the level of Marshmello, Deadmau5, Travis Scott, and Ariana Grande.

The crowd besieges the Nintendo exhibit at the 2018 Electronic Entertainment Expo (E3): the Battle Royale mode of *Fortnite* for the Switch has just been announced.

2011-2021

LEAGUE OF LEGENDS
A CHALLENGE TO THE LAST CLICK

Remember the early 2000s, when you could finally play strategy games online in real time—games like *Company of Heroes* (2006) and *Warhammer 40,000: Dawn of War* (2004)? Defending your own base while battling against the clock to equip your army and destroy the enemy base was an exciting experience, because you needed to learn effective tactics to balance defense and offense. Those games evolved into to the MOBAs of today, of which *League of Legends* (2009) is currently the dominant title.

To what does this complicated and punishingly difficult game—which for years lacked a good tutorial—owe its extraordinary success? Perhaps the answer lies in its very difficulty. Yes, it takes hours just to get the hang of what you're doing. And no matter how good you are, it's still extremely easy to let down your team. A forty-minute game can still end in a crushing and undeserved defeat. And yet—these seemingly impossible challenges are exactly why players stay hooked.

A player in a *League of Legends* tournament at Torino Comics 2018.

VIRTUAL REALITY
THE FINAL FRONTIER?

Technological advances have always played a key role in the history of video games—and they have brought us ever closer to the goal of total immersion. In this respect, virtual reality may represent the final frontier. In the 1980s, the term "virtual reality" sounded like science fiction, and in the 1990s, timid and underwhelming experiments soured users on the idea. But a sea change occurred in 2016. That year, after a long period of research

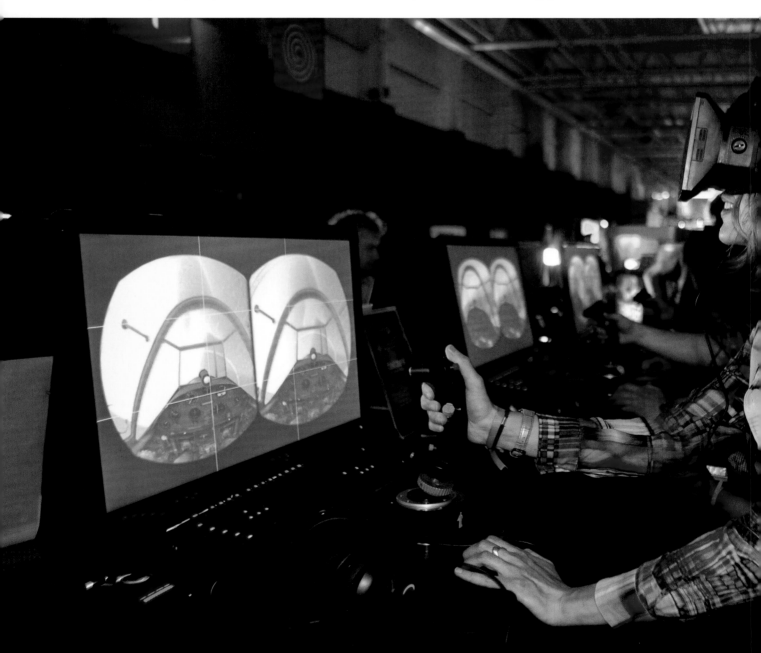

and fitful progress, multiple developers put new VR goggles on the market. On the PC front, HTC Vive and Oculus Rift offered engaging experiences, if you had a high-performance gaming computer. Among the consoles, only Sony seriously took on virtual reality, with the PlayStation VR add-on for the PlayStation 4. This took the form of a headset connected to the console and assisted by PlayStation Move commands and the PlayStation Eye camera. It was meant to give the user 360-degree immersion in the game, but the results were disappointing: while the graphics were fluid, their quality still left much to be desired. The small number of noteworthy titles and the high cost of the equipment prevented PlayStation VR from being widely adopted. But the potential of VR is still there to be realized.

The screen duplicates the stereo image of the Oculus Rift, one of the more engaging VR systems for the PC.

2011—2021

NINTH GENERATION

IMAGINATION BECOMES REALITY

Playing through the pandemic: it may seem strange, but the role of the video game was never more important than in 2020–21. Locked down at home, separated physically, millions of people sought a little human comfort through their consoles, smartphones, and PCs. This explains the success of titles based on the idea of community, like *Animal Crossing: New Horizons*, which sold eleven million copies in twelve days, and why the PlayStation 5 and the Xbox Series X/S sold out before they were even released. The ninth generation of consoles brought the immersive DualSense controller, the almost perfect virtual worlds of *Assassin's Creed Valhalla*, enchanted dungeon crawlers like *Hades*, and the explosion of e-sports, with the emergence of super-teams in several countries. Thinking about all the changes that video games have already undergone, it is easy to get lost in nostalgia. Is retrogaming the future of gaming?

THE PANDEMIC AND GAMING

In March 2020, when news anchors began talking about COVID-19 and how the new virus was rapidly spreading throughout the world, those who had played *Plague Inc.* (2012) knew exactly what was happening and how the situation could unfold. This simulation and strategy video game from Ndemic Creations offers two different ways to play. In the first, you play as the pathogen, and you must destroy the world population before a cure is found. In the second, you must contain the spread of the pandemic with quarantines and restrictions and develop a vaccine as soon as possible, while facing citizen revolts if your measures are too stringent. All of this was eerily close to what actually happened. And yet, it was because of its prophetic powers that the video game sector grew stronger during this tragic year, while other parts of the economy foundered. It is estimated that one in two Americans played video games during lockdown. Sales in 2020 reached almost $180 billion worldwide, up 20 percent from 2019. The ninth-generation consoles posted incredible sales numbers, with the PlayStation 5 and the Xbox Series X/S selling out even in their preorder periods.

James Vaughan shows off a screenshot of *Plague Inc.* (2012), which anticipated the later Ebola and COVID-19 epidemics.

SEEKING COMMUNITY THROUGH GAMING

[N] intendo's *Animal Crossing: New Horizons* came out in March 2020 and sold more than eleven million copies in just twelve days. This title, which was based on the idea of community and invited people to come together to build and interact, is a prime example of how COVID-19 influenced gaming. The surge in sales and the desire to connect were the principal features of gaming during the pandemic. Even if the classic online FPS and MOBA games saw few changes during lockdown (except maybe crowded servers), there was a significant increase in the number of so-called casual gamers, who play occasionally and favor more relaxing titles, like *Animal Crossing*.

A life-size character from *Animal Crossing: New Horizons* welcomes visitors to the Nintendo store in Shibuya, Tokyo.

SPIDER-MAN
INTO THE SPIDER-VERSE

ONLY ON THE BIG SCREEN CHRISTMAS

SPIDER-MAN: MILES MORALES

When Peter Parker goes on vacation, he leaves his young apprentice Miles Morales to take care of New York. Based on the solid foundations of the first Spider-Man title developed by Insomniac Games (*Marvel's Spider-Man*, 2018), *Spider-Man: Miles Morales* (2020) presents a Big Apple splendidly covered with snow, Christmas cheer, and state-of-the-art graphic brilliance. But the improvements are not only aesthetic. The young Spider-Man has a few more powers at his disposal than Peter Parker did, and these are ably adapted to the new game mechanics enhanced by the PlayStation 5's DualSense controller.

DUALSENSE: INCREASED IMMERSION

Years from now, the PS5's DualSense controller will likely be remembered as one of the most important innovations of the ninth-generation consoles. The DualSense is an incredible input device, perhaps the most tangible example of the "next-generation" play promised by the new wave of consoles. At first glance, it may look similar to previous Sony controllers, but the DualSense actually changes to match the gameplay, thanks to the magic of its adaptive analog triggers: the game itself can make the triggers easier or harder to pull based on the scenario or action. Immersion is also increased by the DualSense's greater fidelity in reproducing vibration. It's exciting to feel the rumble of a train or the crackling of electricity for the first time in *Spider-Man: Miles Morales*, thanks to the controller's tactile feedback. The DualSense has taught us that the way forward for controllers is not in adding more buttons, but in offering a deeper and richer experience.

OPPOSITE: Teenage Miles Morales is the hero of the movie *Spider-Man: Into the Spider-Verse* (2018) and the video game *Spider-Man: Miles Morales* (2020).

FOLLOWING PAGES: At left, Sony's new PlayStation 5. At right, its nemesis, the Xbox Series X from Microsoft.

HIKIKOMORI
EXTREME ISOLATION

The virtual world is becoming ever more attractive, and the ability to interact with other players on gaming platforms in some ways creates a reality parallel to everyday life. According to some studies, players are attracted to MMOs by the opportunity to interact with other users and challenge themselves against real adversaries. But they are also fascinated by the pleasure of immersing themselves in an imaginary environment. When this phenomenon spins out of control, it can lead to a type of extreme social isolation called *hikikomori*, a Japanese word that literally means "to point inward and become confined." Those who suffer from this real syndrome reject real life, isolating themselves at home and participating only in virtual social relationships. Not coincidentally, the concept was coined in Japan, where social pressures are so high that children often suffer from stress even before adolescence. The *hikikomori* phenomenon has been seen as a form of passive rebellion against the family and related social and cultural expectations. Given that the virtual world is seen as a refuge, it is easy to point at video games as a cause of social isolation among young people. Naturally, similar accusations are leveled against social media, movies, and music. . . .

Hikikomori (2021), written and directed by Sophie Attelann, is one of several movies about the *hikikomori* phenomenon that began in Japan in the 1980s. It portrays the solitude of virtual relationships.

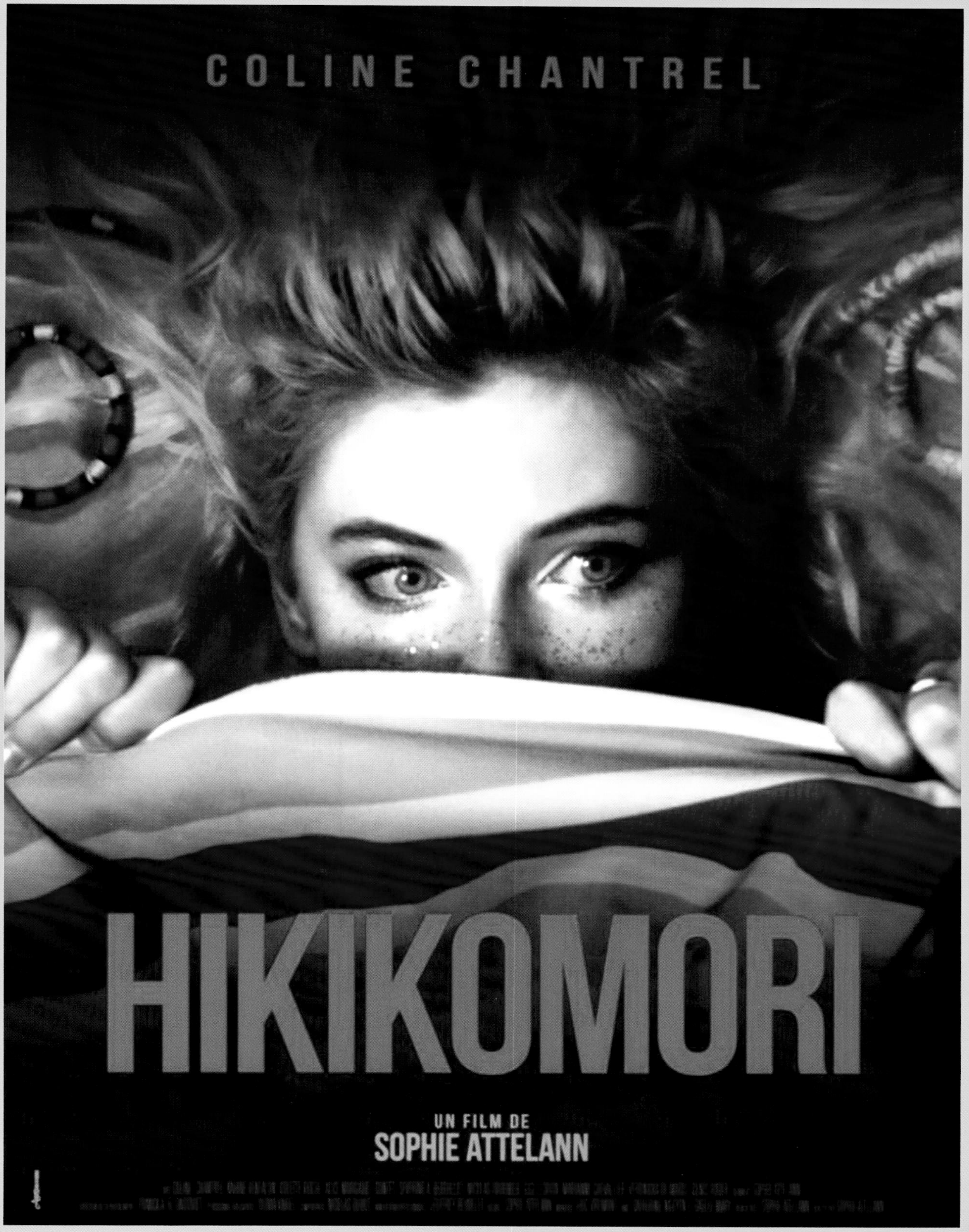
COLINE CHANTREL
HIKIKOMORI
UN FILM DE
SOPHIE ATTELANN

ASSASSIN'S CREED VALHALLA
EXPLORATIONS AND VIKING RAIDS

With an apparently infinite world to explore and a similarly extensive series of missions to accomplish, Eivor, the protagonist of *Assassin's Creed Valhalla* (2020), can still make time to admire each blade of grass and distant mountain. Thanks to the power of the hardware in the Xbox Series X/S and PlayStation 5, loading times are almost nonexistent, and the player is catapulted into a world that is practically perfect in every detail. It takes hundreds of hours to accomplish every mission, kill every enemy, mount a siege, and explore and plunder the open world of this outstanding installment of a legendary series.

Eivor, the protagonist of *Assassin's Creed Valhalla*. In addition to physical combat, the player can engage in *flyting*, or insult contests—displays of rhetorical ability almost reminiscent of those in *Monkey Island*.

The Canadians Guillaume Patry and Victor Martyn were *StarCraft* world champions at the beginning of the millennium, and were real heroes in South Korea, one of the biggest video game markets.

THE GOLDEN AGE OF E-SPORTS

Today, video gaming is also a sport. That is, an e-sport. This is video gaming at a professional level, played not only in virtual arenas but also in real ones, with thousands of spectators. As we have seen, the first official *Space Invaders* tournament in 1980, with its 10,000 participants, launched this type of competition. Ten years later, the first Nintendo World Championships were held. But it's the Red Annihilation *Quake* tournament of 1997 that is remembered as the first real e-sports event. Dennis "Thresh" Fong emerged as the winner from among nearly 2,000 entrants and won *Quake* creator John Carmack's Ferrari 328. The advent of the Internet, the game *StarCraft* (1998), and the platform Battle.net ushered in the era of online competitions. The sequel, *StarCraft II* (2010), improved the gameplay of this space-themed masterpiece of the real-time strategy genre. Currently, the Global StarCraft II League (GSL) in South Korea is considered the most prestigious, with more than 17.5 million views on Twitch alone.

THE BIGGEST TOURNAMENTS + THE STRONGEST TEAMS

At the beginning of the new millennium, important international tournaments were launched, such as the World Cyber Games (2000), the Electronic Sports World Cup (2003), and Major League Gaming (2002), which today is the biggest e-sports league and the one with the most generous prizes. Dominant teams emerged, like Newbee (China), FaZe Clan (United States), Astralis (Denmark), Team Liquid (Netherlands), and Fnatic (UK). As the overall gaming market has grown, so have e-sports. According to data from the Global Esports & Live Streaming Market Report, e-sports have already surpassed $1 billion in annual revenue.

Fnatic is among the strongest teams in the world, along with Newbee, FaZe Clan, Astralis, and Team Liquid.

HADES
FROM THE UNDERWORLD TO THE TOP OF THE CHARTS

It is unusual for an independent production like *Hades* (2020), from Supergiant Games, to win a string of awards. Carefully refined during a long early-access period, this sophisticated and sexy dungeon crawler has cast a spell on players, first on the Nintendo Switch and later on the PlayStation 5 and other platforms. In the role of Zagreus, son of Hades, the player must try to escape the underworld again and again, facing randomly generated challenges and winning various rewards. The action is well balanced and the character development is deep and interesting, as is the apparently bottomless well of the story, which advances along with the gameplay. *Hades* is a true modern classic.

London, MCM Comic Con 2021: a cosplayer portrays Thanatos, a character from *Hades*. This game became a pop culture phenomenon, even though it was an indie production.

2020—

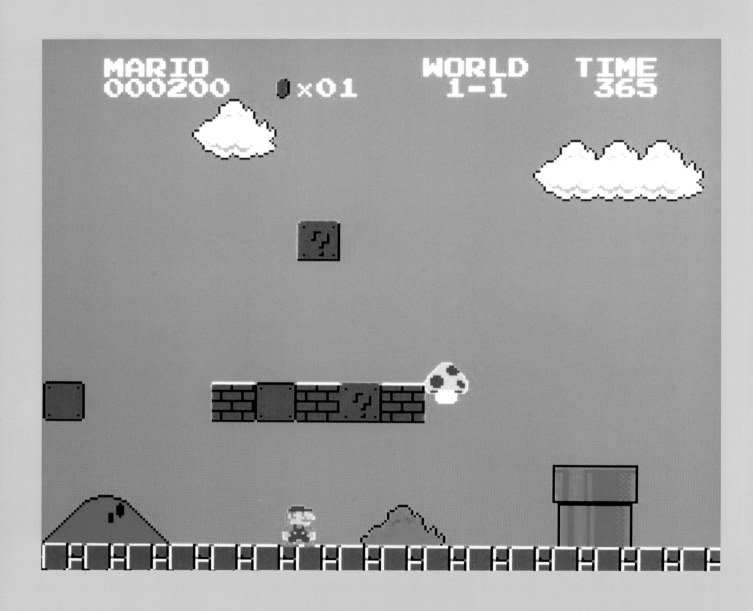

RETROGAMING
MORE THAN COLLECTING

More than fifty years have passed since the first video games came out. Video games are still one of the newest mass media, and yet they have already undergone an exponential technological and economic development. The evolution of gaming is conventionally measured by the release of successive generations of consoles and, of course, by the iconic games that everyone remembers. But the 2010s saw the emergence of a nostalgic phenomenon called retrogaming. Collecting the consoles and games of previous generations became a widespread pursuit, and fans began to seek out rare and historic items. The most passionate collectors acquire only perfectly working consoles and cartridges, well preserved and with their original boxes.

But is retrogaming just collecting, or is it also a way to preserve the experience of the past? Many fans will say that it is much more satisfying to play historic titles on the original consoles than on a cold computer emulator. It is also true that the market for retrogaming collectibles has become a real business and achieved unbelievable prices: as we have seen, the only surviving prototype of the Nintendo PlayStation sold for $360,000 at auction. And a rare copy of *Super Mario Bros.* sold for $2 million!

A screenshot of the first level of *Super Mario Bros.* Mario is the only video game character with a day dedicated to him. Since the 1990s, his fans have celebrated Mario Day on March 10, which can be abbreviated as "Mar10."

WHAT IS THE FUTURE OF GAMING?

It seems almost unbelievable that video games have become a $200 million industry, dwarfing movies and music. Yet, just fifty years on, video games are one of the leading sectors of the global economy, and some observers maintain that this is only the beginning. But what can we expect from the future? Technical development benefits gaming, and as we have seen, virtual reality has long seemed poised to play an important role in video games.

Potentially, it could allow players to "live" inside an interactive and immersive 3D world. In recent years, artificial intelligence has also made significant steps forward, particularly in language processing. Voice recognition and open dialogue with computers could kick off a new chapter for video games, especially if combined with virtual reality. For example, non-player characters could respond intelligently and naturally to questions and commands. In first-person shooters, sports games, and strategy games, players could control the action with their voices as well as with gamepads. The future of video games is still unfolding, but whatever happens, it will definitely be entertaining.

A Meta Oculus Quest 2 headset. Virtual reality, combined with artificial intelligence, could be an essential element of video games in the future.

2020–

INDEX

PHOTO CREDITS

p. 4: Fraser Kerr Photography / Shutterstock, Inc.; pp. 6-7: Estate of Keith Morris / Redferns / Getty Images; pp. 14-15: Ian Hubball / Alamy Stock Photo; p. 18: Universal History Archive / UIG via Getty Images; p. 21: Courtesy the Arcade Flyer Archive; pp. 22-23: Mirrorpix / Getty Images; pp. 28-29: Bettmann / Partner; p. 30, top: Staff / AFP via Getty Images; p. 30, bottom: Screenshot via MobyGames; p. 31: Chris Rand / Georgfotoart / Wikimedia Commons; pp. 32-33: Bettmann / Getty Images; p. 34: Screenshot via MobyGames; p. 35: Courtesy the Arcade Flyer Archive; p. 36: Courtesy the Arcade Flyer Archive; p. 40: ArcadeImages / Alamy Stock Photo; p. 41: Screenshot via MobyGames; p. 42: Courtesy the Arcade Flyer Archive; p. 44, top: Screenshot via MobyGames; pp. 52-53: Denver Post via Getty Images; p. 67, bottom: Screenshot via MobyGames; pp. 72-73: Ralf-Finn Hestoft / Corbis via Getty Images; p. 74: Bryan Bedder / Stringer via Getty Images; p. 75: Screenshot via MobyGames; p. 77: Philippe Martin / Rog01 / Wikimedia Commons; p. 97: Conker's Bad Fur Day / nintendo.fandom.com; p. 100: INTERFOTO / Alamy Stock Photo; pp. 102-3: Bill Bertram / Wikimedia Commons; p. 107, top: ArcadeImages / Alamy Stock Photo; p. 107: ZUMA Press, Inc. / Alamy Stock Photo; p. 112: Screenshot via MobyGames; p. 114: Maxis Software Inc. / copyrighted screenshot / fair use; pp. 122-23: Courtesy the Arcade Flyer Archive; p. 128: Screenshot via MobyGames; p. 129: Maurice Savage / Alamy Stock Photo; p. 130: Evan Amos / Wikimedia Commons; p. 131: Screenshot via MobyGames; p. 133, top: Evan Amos / Wikimedia Commons; p. 133, bottom: Thngs / Wikimedia Commons; p. 143: ArcadeImages / Alamy Stock Photo; p. 145: Alex Segre / Alamy Stock Photo; p. 147: Screenshot via MobyGames; pp. 148-49: Evan Amos / Wikimedia Commons; pp. 150: Altan Dilan / Wikimedia Commons; p. 151: Screenshot via MobyGames; p. 153: Matteo Pedrini / Wikimedia Commons; pp. 154-55: Evan Amos / Wikimedia Commons; p. 158: Jemal Countess / Stringer via Getty Images; pp. 160-61: Dmitrii Pridannikov / Alamy Stock Photo; pp. 162-63: Evan Amos / Wikimedia Commons; pp. 164-65: Evan Amos / Wikimedia Commons; p. 166: Screenshot via MobyGames; p. 168, top: Screenshot via MobyGames; p. 168, bottom: PA Images/Alamy Stock Photo; pp. 171: Evan Amos / Wikimedia Commons; pp. 172-73: Courtesy Supergiant Games; pp. 176-77: PA Images / Alamy Stock Photo; pp. 180-81, top: Ian Dagnall / Alamy Stock Photo; p. 181, bottom: Dimple Patel / Alamy Stock Photo; pp. 182-183: Takimata / Tokyoship / Wikimedia Commons; p. 187: Getty Images / Bob Riha, Jr.; p. 190: Screenshot via MobyGames; pp. 192-93: Bruce Liu / Wikimedia Commons; pp. 194-95: Sergey Galyonkin / Wikimedia Commons; p. 196: Nicolò Campo / Alamy Stock Photo; pp. 198-99: Mehdi Chebil / Alamy Stock Photo; p. 202: Leon Neal / AFP via Getty Images; p. 203: ZUMA Press, Inc. / Alamy Stock Photo; p. 204, top: BFA / Alamy Stock Photo; p. 204, bottom: Screenshot via MobyGames; p. 209: TCD / Prod. DB / Alamy Stock Photo; pp. 210-11: David Esser / Alamy Stock Photo; pp. 212-13: Kim Jae-Hwan / AFP via Getty Images; pp. 214-15: Chesnot / Getty Images; pp. 216-217: Imageplotter / Alamy Stock Photo; p. 218: pumkinpie / Alamy Stock Photo; p. 220-221: Joan Cros / NurPhoto via Getty Images.

Thanks to Andrea Gallione for the photos on pages 125, 126, and 142.

All other photos belong to Nuinui SA, and picture items from the collection of the Videogame Art Museum, Bologna. Photography by Giuseppe Matera.